The Prepper's Canning & Preserving Bible

The Essential Guide Water Bath & Pressure Canning, Fermenting, Dehydrating, Pickling to Stockpiling Food for Long-Term Survival

By Steve Halone

Table Of Contents

FOREWORD   13

A Personal Journey into the World of Self-Sufficiency   13

INTRODUCTION   17

The Rising Importance of Self-Sufficiency in the 21st Century   17

Overview of Canning and Preserving: A Historical Perspective   19

Safety Protocols and Hygiene in Home Canning   21

BOOK I: FOUNDATIONS OF CANNING AND PRESERVING   25

Essential Equipment and Their Uses   25

Selecting Quality Ingredients for Optimal Preservation   27

Basic Techniques: Cleaning, Preparing, and Sterilizing   28

BOOK II: WATER BATH CANNING   31

Introduction to Water Bath Canning: Principles and Practices   31

Step-by-Step Guide: Jams, Jellies, and Marmalades   33
    Mango & Saffron Marmalade   33
    Spiced Blueberry Jam   33
    Ginger-Pear Jelly   34
    Raspberry-Lavender Jam   34
    Blackberry-Chia Seed Jam   35
    Apricot-Rosemary Jelly   35
    Cherry-Almond Preserve   36
    Orange-Cinnamon Marmalade   36
    Strawberry-Basil Jam   37
    Fig and Vanilla Bean Jam   37
    Pomegranate-Ginger Jelly   38
    Peach-Thyme Jam   38
    Kiwi-Lime Preserve   39
    Pineapple-Cilantro Jam   39
    Plum-Star Anise Jam   40
    Grapefruit-Rose Jelly   40
    Apple-Cinnamon Butter   41
    Red Currant-Chile Jelly   41

Lemon-Basil Marmalade 42
Blackcurrant-Vanilla Jam 42

Preserving Fruits and Tomatoes: From Orchard to Jar 43
Spiced Peach Slices 43
Tomato Basil Sauce 43
Brandied Cherries 44
Honeyed Pear Preserves 44
Apple Cider Compote 45
Lemon-Preserved Figs 45
Zesty Orange Marmalade 46
Spicy Tomato Chutney 46
Vanilla-Infused Plums 47
Rustic Grape Jam 47
Cinnamon-Spiced Applesauce 48
Sweet Cherry Preserve 48
Fiery Peppered Tomato Relish 49
Mulled Wine Grapes 49
Gingered Pear Chutney 50
Balsamic Strawberry Compote 50
Lemony Fig Spread 51
Vanilla Bean Peaches 51
Spicy Tomato Salsa 52
Bourbon-Infused Cherries 52

Acidic Foods Canning: Pickles, Relishes, and Chutneys 53
Spiced Cauliflower Pickles 53
Mango-Lime Chutney 53
Dill Garlic Cucumbers 54
Carrot and Ginger Relish 54
Sweet and Spicy Zucchini Pickles 55
Green Tomato Chutney 55
Hot Jalapeño Relish 56
Red Onion Marmalade 56
Bell Pepper and Apple Chutney 57
Classic Bread and Butter Pickles 57
Cranberry-Orange Relish 58
Spicy Corn Relish 58
Pear and Ginger Chutney 59
Beetroot and Onion Pickle 59
Cucumber and Mint Chutney 60
Garlic Dill Green Beans 60
Apple-Cider Vinegar Onions 61
Lemon and Rosemary Olives 61
Sweet Pepper Jam 62
Tamarind Date Chutney 62

BOOK III: PRESSURE CANNING   **65**

Understanding Pressure Canning: The Science and Method   **65**

Canning Vegetables and Soups: A Comprehensive Guide   **67**
Hearty Vegetable Soup   67
Classic Beef Stew   67
Spiced Carrot Soup   69
Chicken Noodle Soup   69
Tomato Basil Soup   70
Lentil Soup with Vegetables   70
Split Pea and Ham Soup   71
Creamy Potato Soup   71
Vegetable Minestrone   72
Corn and Chicken Chowder   72
Rustic Beef Barley Soup   73
Chunky Vegetable Broth   73
Curried Lentil Soup   74
Italian Minestrone with Pasta   74
Savory Mushroom Soup   75
Spicy Black Bean Soup   75
Cream of Asparagus Soup   76
Potato Leek Soup   76
Chicken and Vegetable Stew   77
Butternut Squash Soup   77
Chicken Soup Base   78
Spicy Sausage and Peppers   78
Herb-Infused Pork Chops   79
Turkey Chili   79
Curried Lamb Stew   80
Shrimp Creole   80
Beef Bourguignon   81
Venison Stew   81
Seafood Bisque   82
Braised Rabbit with Vegetables   82
Classic Duck Confit   83
Italian Sausage and Peppers   83
Asian Pork Belly   84
Mexican Chicken Tinga   84
Moroccan Lamb Tagine   85
Herbed Chicken Thighs   85
Savory Turkey Chili   86
Pork Carnitas   86
Asian-Style Beef Ribs   87

Combining Foods: Creating Balanced Meals in a Jar   **88**

Moroccan Chickpea and Vegetable Stew 88

Beef and Barley Soup 88

Chicken Curry with Vegetables 89

Vegetarian Quinoa Chili 89

Tuscan White Bean and Kale Soup 90

Seafood Paella 90

Pork and Sweet Potato Stew 91

Spicy Lentil and Sausage Soup 91

Ratatouille 92

Beef Goulash 92

Chicken Tagine with Apricots 93

Vegetarian Borscht 94

Coq au Vin 94

Spicy Bean and Rice Burrito Filling 95

Thai Green Curry with Chicken 95

Seafood Gumbo 96

Jambalaya 96

Pork and Beans 97

Mediterranean Lamb Stew 97

Southwest Chicken and Corn Chowder 98

BOOK IV: ALTERNATIVE PRESERVATION METHODS **100**

Fermenting Foods: Health Benefits and Basic Recipes **100**

Classic Sauerkraut 101

Kimchi 101

Kombucha 102

Fermented Carrot Sticks 102

Sourdough Starter 103

Ginger Bug (for Homemade Sodas) 103

Beet Kvass 104

Lacto-Fermented Lemons 104

Fermented Hot Sauce 105

Miso Fermented Vegetables 105

Fermented Garlic Honey 106

Pineapple Tepache 106

Fermented Cranberry Sauce 107

Traditional Russian Kvass 107

Fermented Mango Chutney 108

Water Kefir 108

Japanese Natto 109

Fermented Sriracha Sauce 109

Cultured Mustard 110

Fermented Beet Kvass 110

Dehydrating Fruits, Vegetables, and Meats: Techniques and Tips **111**

Crispy Apple Chips 112
Sweet Potato Dog Treats 112
Spicy Beef Jerky 113
Zesty Lemon Zest 113
Herb-Infused Tomato Slices 114
Homemade Banana Chips 114
Spicy Kale Chips 115
Savory Mushroom Powder 115
Dried Pineapple Rings 116
Venison Jerky 116
Ginger-Infused Pear Slices 117
Dried Chili Flakes 117
Garlic and Herb Seasoned Tomatoes 118
Citrus Peel Powder 118
Dried Mango Slices 119
Crunchy Green Bean Snacks 119
Dried Strawberry Slices 119
Turkey Jerky Strips 120
Dried Blueberries 120
Spiced Carrot Chips 121

Pickling: Beyond Cucumbers - Exploring Variety ... **122**
Spiced Carrot Pickles 122
Sweet and Tangy Red Onion Pickles 122
Garlic Dill Green Beans 123
Asian-Style Pickled Mushrooms 123
Pickled Beets with Cinnamon 124
Sweet Chili Cauliflower Pickles 124
Fiery Jalapeño Pickles 125
Pickled Rainbow Peppers 125
Ginger-Pickled Daikon Radish 126
Pickled Cherry Tomatoes 126
Spicy Pickled Okra 127
Sweet Pickled Red Cabbage 127
Pickled Asparagus Spears 128
Pickled Ginger (Gari) 128
Pickled Pearl Onions 129
Pickled Yellow Squash 129
Pickled Radishes with Peppercorns 130
Pickled Green Peppers 130
Curried Pickled Cauliflower 131
Pickled Fennel with Citrus 131

Smoking and Curing Meats: Traditional and Modern Methods ... **132**
Classic Smoked Brisket 132
Applewood Smoked Chicken 132
Hickory-Smoked Pork Ribs 132

Maple-Cured Bacon 133

Cold-Smoked Salmon 134

Smoked Beef Jerky 134

Smoked Gouda Cheese 135

Peppercorn-Crusted Smoked Duck 135

Country-Style Smoked Sausages 136

Apple Cider Cured Ham 136

Smoked Turkey Legs 137

Spiced Pastrami 137

Garlic and Herb Smoked Pork Loin 138

Maple Smoked Bacon 138

Hickory Smoked Venison Jerky 139

Smoked Duck Breast 139

Smoked Andouille Sausage 140

Cured and Smoked Lamb Ribs 140

Cold Smoked Cheese 141

Smoked Trout 141

Book V: Advanced Preservation and Storage **144**

Building a Varied and Nutritious Prepper's Pantry **144**

Long-Term Storage Techniques: Vacuum Sealing, Freezing, and More ... **146**

Seasonal and Bulk Canning: Strategies for Year-Round Preparation ... **147**

Book VI: Special Topics and Recipes **150**

Special Dietary Considerations: Low-Sugar, Low-Salt, and Allergen-Free Recipes ... **150**

Golden Harvest Apple Butter 150

Summer Zucchini Relish 150

Rustic Pear Preserve 152

Garden Veggie Salsa 152

Tangy Cranberry Sauce 153

Roasted Red Pepper Spread 153

Savory Mushroom Pâté 154

Cinnamon Apple Chutney 154

Balsamic Onion Marmalade 155

Lemon-Thyme Jelly 155

Beetroot and Ginger Chutney 156

Spicy Green Tomato Salsa 156

Carrot and Orange Marmalade 157

Minted Pea Spread 157

Pickled Rainbow Chard Stems 158

Raspberry and Rosewater Jam 158

Savory Pumpkin Butter 159

Sun-Dried Tomato Tapenade   159
Apple and Cranberry Chutney   160
Garlic Dill Pickles   160
Strawberry Rhubarb Compote   161
Pickled Red Onions   161
Apricot Vanilla Spread   162
Basil Pesto   162
Spicy Carrot Chutney   163
Mixed Berry Jam   163
Savory Eggplant Relish   164
Pear and Ginger Preserve   164
Sweet Pepper Jelly   165

International Preserves: Exploring Global Canning Recipes   **166**
Moroccan Preserved Lemons   166
Indian Mango Chutney   166
Japanese Umeboshi (Pickled Plums)   167
Italian Marinated Artichokes   167
French Ratatouille Preserve   168
Mexican Salsa Verde   168
British Bramble Jelly   169
Greek Olive Tapenade   169
Korean Kimchi   170
South African Chakalaka   170
Spanish Escabeche of Mackerel   171
Thai Sweet Chili Sauce   171
Chinese Plum Sauce   172
Turkish Eggplant Pickle   172
German Sauerkraut   173
Brazilian Pepper Sauce   173
Russian Dill Pickles   174
Filipino Atchara (Pickled Papaya)   174
Middle Eastern Fig Jam   175
Hungarian Pepper and Tomato Relish (Lecsó)   175
Caribbean Pineapple Jam   176
Swedish Lingonberry Preserve   176
Egyptian Lemon and Mint Jelly   177
Peruvian Aji Amarillo Sauce   177
Australian Lemon Myrtle Marmalade   178
Polish Dill Pickle Soup Concentrate   178
Indonesian Sambal Oelek   179
Korean Pear and Ginger Jam   179
Bulgarian Rose Petal Jam   180
Lebanese Pickled Turnips   180

Sweet and Savory Spreads: Expanding Your Flavor Palette   **181**
Roasted Red Pepper Hummus   181

Blackberry Lavender Butter 181
Caramelized Onion and Fig Spread 182
Bourbon Peach Preserve 182
Creamy Herb Cheese Spread 183
Maple Pumpkin Butter 183
Jalapeño Apple Jelly 184
Balsamic Fig and Olive Tapenade 184
Sun-Dried Tomato and Basil Pesto 185
Apple and Cinnamon Butter 185
Raspberry and Rose Jam 186
Garlic and Herb Cheese Spread 186
Pear and Vanilla Bean Jam 187
Spiced Carrot Spread 187
Blueberry Lavender Butter 188
Mint and Pea Pesto 188
Cherry and Almond Conserve 189
Smoky Eggplant Spread 189
Spicy Mango Chutney 190
Fig and Port Wine Jam 190
Roasted Garlic Aioli 191
Cranberry Orange Relish 191
Beetroot and Horseradish Spread 192
Green Tomato and Apple Chutney 192
Zucchini and Lemon Marmalade 193
Pumpkin Spice Spread 193
Black Olive Tapenade 194
Pear and Saffron Chutney 194
Caramel Apple Butter 195
Savory Bacon Jam 195

Preserving Herbs and Spices: Oils, Vinegars, and Infusions **196**
Rosemary Infused Olive Oil 196
Lemon and Thyme Vinegar 196
Spicy Garlic Chili Oil 197
Basil and Pine Nut Pesto Oil 197
Herb Infused Vinegar Mix 198
Citrus Zest Olive Oil 198
Vanilla Bean and Cinnamon Oil 199
Hot Pepper Vinegar 199
Mint and Lemon Balm Tincture 200
Savory Sage and Rosemary Oil 200
Chive Blossom Vinegar 201
Oregano and Garlic Olive Oil 201
Ginger and Turmeric Infusion 202
Cilantro Lime Vinegar 202
Fennel Seed and Orange Oil 203

Rose and Peppercorn Vinegar 203
Lemongrass and Ginger Oil 204
Tarragon and Mustard Seed Vinegar 204
Basil and Lemon Balm Vinegar 205
Spiced Apple Cider Vinegar 205
Dill and Lemon Infused Oil 206
Coriander Seed Vinegar 206
Mint and Cucumber Vinegar 207
Thyme Infused Balsamic Vinegar 207
Garlic and Rosemary Oil 208
Szechuan Pepper Oil 208
Chilli and Lime Vinegar 209
Cardamom and Orange Infused Oil 209
Basil and Garlic Vinegar 210
Sage and Walnut Oil 210

BOOK VII: PRACTICAL APPLICATIONS FOR EVERYDAY LIFE 212

Meal Planning and Preparation with Preserved Foods 212

Emergency Preparedness: Strategies for Building a Resilient Food Supply 213

Community Engagement: Sharing Skills and Resources 215

CONCLUSION 218

The Future of Home Canning and Preserving 218

Continuing Education: Resources and Communities for Enthusiasts 220

APPENDIX 224

Troubleshooting Guide for Common Canning Issues 224

Comprehensive Resource Directory for Supplies and Further Learning 227

Detailed Glossary of Canning and Preserving Terms 230

INDEX 234

ABBREVIATIONS 239

MEASUREMENT CONVERSION TABLE 240

Foreword

A Personal Journey into the World of Self-Sufficiency

In the sprawling tapestry of modern existence, where the hum of technology and the pulse of progress dictate the rhythm of our days, I found myself pausing, pondering the path less trodden - a journey back to the roots, to the essence of self-reliance. This narrative is not merely a recounting of skills acquired or techniques mastered; it is a chronicle of transformation, a heart-felt odyssey into the realm of self-sufficiency through the age-old art of canning and preserving.

My venture into this world was born not from whimsy but necessity, a response to the echoing uncertainties that shroud our contemporary world. Amidst the clatter of global upheavals and the ebb and flow of economic tides, the question loomed large: How could I anchor my family in a haven of safety and sustenance? The answer, I discovered, lay in the time-honored practice of canning and preserving, a beacon guiding me toward self-sufficiency.

The journey commenced in the quietude of my kitchen, amidst the familiar clatter of pots and pans, a space that transformed from a mere area for meal preparation into a crucible of creativity and sustenance. The process of canning, often perceived as a relic of bygone days, revealed itself to be an art form, a dance of flavors and textures, a melding of tradition and innovation. It was here, amongst the steam and the scents of simmering fruits, that I began to weave the tapestry of my own self-reliance.

The initial forays into canning were modest - simple recipes, familiar fruits, and vegetables, the basics of water bath canning. Yet, with each jar sealed and stored, a sense of accomplishment burgeoned within me. The rows of jars, lined like sentinels on my pantry shelves, were not just containers of food; they were symbols of resilience, tangible proof of my capability to nourish and sustain.

As my skills in canning and preserving grew, so did my understanding of their profound significance. This was not just a culinary pursuit; it was an act of preservation, not only of food but of a way of life that respects the rhythms of nature the bounty of the earth, and the value of manual labor. Each batch of jam, each jar o pickles, each container of preserved fruit became a testament to the harmony between human endeavor and nature's offerings.

The art of canning and preserving opened my eyes to the beauty of simplicity and the richness of minimalism. In an era where excess is often celebrated, I found joy in the less-is-more philosophy. The act of preserving food became a meditative practice, a time to reflect on consumption, waste, and sustainability. It was a humbling lesson in gratitude, an appreciation for each ingredient, each season, each harvest.

This journey was not without its challenges. The learning curve was steep, the hours long, and the labor intensive. There were moments of doubt, mishaps in the kitchen, and the occasional failed batch. But with each setback came a surge of resilience, a determination to refine my techniques and deepen my understanding.

In the alchemy of canning and preserving, I discovered not just a skill but a passion, a way to connect with my roots, with tradition, and with a community of like-minded individuals. It became a bridge connecting the past with the present, a thread weaving through the fabric of history, culture, and personal growth.

The world of self-sufficiency is vast and varied, a landscape rich with knowledge, skills, and experiences. My journey into canning and preserving is but one path in this expansive terrain, a path that has led me to discover the strength in self-reliance, the joy in simplicity, and the peace in knowing that, come what may, I have the skills to sustain and thrive.

As I pen these words, my kitchen is filled with the aroma of spices and fruits, a sensory reminder of the journey I have embarked upon. The jars on my shelves are more than just food; they are stories, each one a chapter in my ongoing tale of self-sufficiency, a tale that I continue to write with each season's harvest.

Introduction

The Rising Importance of Self-Sufficiency in the 21st Century

In the canvas of the 21st century, woven with threads of technological advancements and global interconnections, there emerges an ironic yet profound resurgence in the quest for self-sufficiency. This revival, seemingly antithetical to the age of digital omnipresence and instant gratifications, speaks volumes about the underlying currents shaping our contemporary ethos. As we stand on the precipice of a new era, the value and relevance of self-sufficiency, particularly in the domain of food preservation, beckons us with renewed urgency and significance.

The concept of self-sufficiency, often romanticized in the annals of pastoral poetry and bucolic narratives, finds its modern incarnation not as an escape but as a necessary response to the multifaceted challenges of our times. Climate change, with its unpredictable weather patterns and impact on agriculture, has cast a looming shadow over food security. Economic fluctuations, global pandemics, and political turmoil have further underscored the fragility of our supply chains, bringing to the forefront the stark realization of our dependencies.

Amidst this backdrop, self-sufficiency emerges as a beacon of empowerment, a tangible solution within the grasp of individuals seeking stability in an unstable world. The art of preserving food, a skill that spans centuries and cultures, stands at the forefront of this movement. It represents not just a method of extending the shelf-life of produce but embodies a holistic approach towards resilience, sustainability, and mindfulness in our consumption practices.

The resurgence of interest in canning and preserving is more than a trend; it is a testament to a collective awakening. Individuals across demographics, from urban dwellers with windowsill herb gardens to rural homesteaders tending to acres of land, are rediscovering the wisdom in these ancient practices. This renewed interest is not a mere nostalgic yearning for the past but a pragmatic adaptation to our present realities, a reclamation of control over what we consume and how we sustain ourselves.

In this journey towards self-reliance, canning and preserving serve as essential skills. They transcend the boundaries of mere culinary activities and morph into acts of resistance against the ephemeral nature of our consumptive patterns. By preserving food, we extend the bounty of seasons, reduce waste, and forge a bond with the rhythms of nature. Each jar of preserved fruit, each batch of homemade pickles, is small but significant step towards a more sustainable and self-reliant lifestyle.

The process of preserving food is also an education in patience, an antidote to the instantaneity that pervades modern life. It teaches us to value the time and effort that goes into growing, harvesting, and preparing food. This connection to our food's journey from farm to table instills a sense of gratitude and respect for the natural resources that sustain us. In a world where convenience often trumps quality, canning and preserving stand as reminders of the joy and fulfillment found in slowing down and savoring the fruits of our labor.

Furthermore, the practice of canning and preserving fosters community and connectivity. It revives the tradition of sharing knowledge, recipes, and produce strengthening social bonds and creating a sense of belonging. In times of uncertainty, these communities become invaluable sources of support and collective resilience. They serve as repositories of knowledge, safeguarding skills and traditions that are vital for our sustenance.

As we navigate the complexities of the 21st century, the relevance of self-sufficiency continues to grow. It is not an abandonment of the conveniences of modern life but an integration of traditional wisdom into our contemporary existence. It is a choice to be proactive rather than reactive, to embrace a lifestyle that values sustainability, resilience, and self-reliance.

Overview of Canning and Preserving: A Historical Perspective

To appreciate the art of canning and preserving, we must embark on a voyage through time, tracing the lineage of this ancient practice that has been a cornerstone in the edifice of human civilization. This journey is not merely an academic exploration; it is a narrative woven into the very fabric of our existence, a tale of survival, ingenuity, and cultural evolution.

In the annals of history, the quest to preserve food has been as vital as the quest for food itself. Our ancestors, attuned to the rhythms of nature and the impermanence of seasons, sought methods to extend the bounty of harvests. From the sun-drenched lands of ancient Egypt to the rugged terrains of the Norse, every culture has contributed to the mosaic of preservation techniques, each method a testament to the ingenuity and adaptability of humankind.

The rudimentary forms of preservation employed salting, drying, and fermenting, harnessing the elements of nature to prolong the life of food. These methods were not just practical solutions but were imbued with cultural significance, often intertwined with rituals and traditions that defined the ethos of communities. The art of preserving food was passed down through generations, a legacy of knowledge that laid the foundation for the sophisticated techniques we employ today.

The advent of canning, a relatively recent chapter in this saga, marked a paradigm shift in the history of food preservation. The genesis of modern canning is attributed to the 18th-century French confectioner Nicolas Appert, whose experiments in sealing food in glass jars and subjecting them to heat laid the groundwork for this revolutionary method. This innovation was not born in a vacuum; it was a response to a challenge posed by the French government, seeking a method to preserve food for its army and navy. Appert's success epitomized the fusion of culinary art, scientific inquiry, and societal need, a confluence that has been the hallmark of human progress.

The subsequent refinement and democratization of canning, particularly with the advent of the tin can, transformed food preservation from a domestic art to an industrial marvel. This transition was not just a technological leap; it was a catalyst that reshaped societies. The ability to preserve food for extended periods altered the dynamics of food supply, impacting everything from military campaigns to mass migrations, from urbanization to exploration.

As we trace the evolution of canning and preserving through the Industrial Revolution and into the modern era, we witness a story of ebbs and flows. The two World Wars were periods of heightened reliance on canned foods, a necessity that ingrained the practice in the collective consciousness of societies. The post-war era, with the allure of convenience and the advent of refrigeration, saw a waning in home canning, as the gleam of modernity often overshadowed traditional practices.

Safety Protocols and Hygiene in Home Canning

As we delve into the intricacies of home canning, we must anchor ourselves with an unwavering focus on safety. This emphasis is not born out of fear but out of respect for the process and an understanding of its implications. The act of preserving food is a delicate dance between nature's bounty and our endeavor to extend its longevity. This dance, while beautiful, carries inherent risks if not performed with care and knowledge.

The first cornerstone of safe canning is understanding the science behind it. At its core, canning is a method of creating an environment where harmful bacteria, yeasts, and molds cannot thrive. The process involves heating the food to a temperature that destroys potential pathogens and then sealing it in an airtight container to prevent recontamination. This scientific approach is crucial in ensuring the safety and quality of canned food.

Hygiene, the second cornerstone, is integral to every step of the canning process. It begins with the selection of fresh, high-quality ingredients and extends to every utensil, jar, lid, and surface used. Sterilization of jars and equipment is not just a recommendation; it is a necessity. This meticulous attention to cleanliness helps prevent the introduction of bacteria into the canned goods, safeguarding the health of those who will enjoy them.

Another critical aspect of safe canning is the understanding and adherence to tested recipes and methods. The allure of creativity and experimentation, while a valuable aspect of culinary endeavors, must be tempered with caution in canning. Deviating from established recipes and processes can lead to unsafe products. It's essential to respect the balance of acidity, temperature, and time, as these factors play a crucial role in ensuring food safety.

Furthermore, vigilance must be maintained in the storage and consumption of canned goods. Regular inspection of jars for signs of spoilage, such as bulging lids, off-odors, or discoloration, is crucial. Understanding that safety in canning is not just about the process but also about the aftermath is essential. This ongoing vigilance is a commitment to the well-being of those who partake in the fruits of our labor.

Book I: Foundations Of Canning And Preserving

Essential Equipment and Their Uses

At the heart of this culinary concerto is the canner. It's not just a pot; it's a vessel that holds not only our ingredients but also our aspirations of self-sufficiency. Whether it's a water bath canner for high-acid foods like fruits and pickles or a pressure canner for low-acid foods like vegetables and meats, each serves its purpose in ensuring the food is processed at the correct temperature for the right amount of time. The water bath canner, with its simple design and operation, is a gateway for beginners, a friendly introduction to the world of canning. The pressure canner, on the other hand, is like a trusted sage, indispensable for its ability to reach higher temperatures essential for safely preserving a wider range of foods.

Jars, the receptacles of our endeavors, are not merely containers but time capsules, capturing the freshness and flavor of seasonal produce. They come in various sizes, each suited for different types of food. From the petite jelly jar, perfect for savory spreads and sweet preserves, to the larger quart-sized jars, ideal for fruits and vegetables, the choice of jar size reflects the scale of our culinary ambitions and the needs of our households.

Lids and rings are the unsung heroes in the canning process. Their role might seem passive, but they are the guardians of freshness, the sentinels that ensure a hermetic seal, keeping the outside world at bay and preserving the contents within
in their pristine state.

The jar lifter, a seemingly simple tool, is a talisman against burns and accidents, a reminder that safety is paramount in the canning process. It allows us to handle hot jars with ease and confidence, a small but mighty ally in the kitchen.

The funnel, with its wide mouth tapering down to a narrow end, is a guide, ensuring that the precious produce is safely deposited into jars without spills or waste. It's a bridge between the pot and the jar, an aid in maintaining cleanliness and precision.

Tongs, like extended fingers, offer precision and safety in handling the ingredients. They are the conductors, guiding the food into jars, ensuring each piece is placed with care and intention.

A bubble remover, though a modest tool, plays a crucial role in ensuring the longevity of canned goods. It's a wand that releases trapped air, a safeguard against spoilage and a guardian of quality.

A headspace tool, though unassuming, is vital for the canning process. It measures the space between the food and the lid, ensuring a proper seal, preventing spoilage, and preserving the quality of your canned goods.

A ladle is more than just a scoop; it is an extension of our hands. It serves not just in transferring liquids but in ensuring the right proportions and consistency in each jar.

A clean cloth or towel, the final piece in our canning ensemble, is a symbol of diligence. It is used for wiping rims clean, a seemingly minor act but one that is critical for a good seal. It's a reminder that attention to detail is a key ingredient in the recipe for successful canning.

In the grand performance of canning and preserving, each piece of equipment plays its part in a delicate dance of temperature, timing, and technique. As we acquaint ourselves with these tools, we learn not just their functions but the principles they embody. The canner teaches us patience and respect for process; the jars, the value of preservation; the lids and rings, the importance of sealing and protecting; the jar lifter, the need for safety; the funnel, the art of precision; the tongs, the skill of placement; the bubble remover, the importance of attention to detail; the ladle, the essence of proportion and balance; the cloth, the necessity of cleanliness.

Selecting Quality Ingredients for Optimal Preservation

The quest for quality ingredients extends to examining their physical condition. Loo for fruits and vegetables that are free from bruises, blemishes, and signs of deca These imperfections are not merely cosmetic; they can affect the taste and safety c the preserved food. Freshness is paramount – the fresher the produce, the better th preservation. This quest often leads us to local farmers' markets or, for the fortunat few, to our backyard gardens, where the connection between the soil and ou sustenance is vivid and profound.

In the realm of canning, size matters. Uniformity in size and ripeness among fruit and vegetables ensures even cooking and consistency in flavor and texture. Thi uniformity is not a pursuit of aesthetic perfection but a practical consideration t enhance the quality and shelf life of canned goods.

The journey of ingredient selection is also an exploration of variety. Different varietie of fruits and vegetables have varying levels of acidity, pectin, and sugar, all of whic play critical roles in the preservation process. For instance, the choice between a tar Granny Smith apple and a sweet Honeycrisp can influence the flavor profile and th need for additional sugar or pectin in a recipe. Understanding these nuance transforms the act of canning from a mundane task into a culinary adventure.

Beyond fruits and vegetables, the choice of additional ingredients like sugar, vinega spices, and herbs is equally crucial. These ingredients should complement an enhance the natural flavors of the produce, not overpower them. The quality of these secondary ingredients is just as important as the primary produce. Usin high-quality vinegar, pure cane sugar, and fresh, aromatic spices and herbs ca elevate a simple preserve into a gourmet delight.

The ethos of canning and preserving is grounded in sustainability, and this extends t ingredient selection. Where possible, choose organic and non-GMO produce. Thi choice is a commitment to health – both our own and that of our planet. It's a stan against harmful pesticides and a contribution to biodiversity. By making thes choices, we align our canning practices with a broader philosophy of environmenta stewardship and personal well-being.

In selecting the ingredients for canning, we also select the values we wish to embed in our preserves. These values – freshness, quality, sustainability, and respect for nature's rhythms – are the essence of what makes home canning a deeply rewarding experience. As we fill our jars with carefully chosen fruits and vegetables, we're not just preserving food; we're preserving a connection to the earth, to our communities, and to the traditions that have sustained generations.

Basic Techniques: Cleaning, Preparing, and Sterilizing

The cleaning of jars, lids, and canning equipment is equally paramount. This step ensures that the vessels and tools that will hold and process our food are pristine, setting a clean canvas for our canning endeavors.

After cleaning, we enter the realm of preparation. This stage is where our produce begins its transformation, where the raw becomes the ready. Here, fruits may be pitted and chopped, vegetables may be sliced or diced. This preparation is a thoughtful process, where attention to size and shape ensures uniformity in texture and cooking times. In the peeling of an apple or the snapping of a bean lies a meditation on the beauty and bounty of nature's offerings. The act of preparing the produce is a blend of art and science, where each cut and trim is guided by the recipe's requirements and the produce's inherent qualities.

Sterilization, the final act in this trio, is the guardian of safety in the canning process. It's a step that wields the power of heat to vanquish any lingering microorganisms that might spoil our preserves or compromise their safety. The sterilization of jars and lids is a practice steeped in caution and precision. Jars are typically submerged in boiling water, a bath that ensures every nook and cranny is freed from potential contaminants. This process is not just a precaution; it is a critical step that underpins the reliability and trustworthiness of the entire canning process.

In the domain of canning, the importance of timing cannot be overstated. The sterilization process is meticulously timed to ensure effectiveness, a balance between thoroughness and preserving the integrity of the jars and lids. This timing is not just a measure of minutes or seconds; it is a rhythm that aligns with the cadence of safe canning practices.

Equally important in this process is the handling of sterilized equipment. Once th jars and lids have been sterilized, they must be handled with care to prever recontamination. This handling is a dance of delicacy and precision, where tools lik jar lifters and tongs become extensions of our hands, ensuring that the sterility of th equipment is maintained until it is time to fill them with our prepared produce.

Book II: Water Bath Canning

Introduction to Water Bath Canning: Principles and Practices

Water bath canning is the process of preserving high-acid foods in jars using boiling water. This method is ideal for fruits, tomatoes, pickles, jams, jellies, and other preserves with high acidity. The essence of water bath canning lies in its ability to use heat to kill off harmful microorganisms, while the airtight seal of the jar prevents any new ones from entering and spoiling the food. It's a ballet of temperature and time, a delicate balance that ensures the safety and longevity of the food within.

The principle that underpins water bath canning is simple yet profound: heat is used to create a vacuum seal in the canning jars, and this seal prevents air and microorganisms from contaminating the food. When the jars are placed in boiling water, the contents of the jars expand, and air is forced out of the jars. As the jars cool after being removed from the water, the contents contract, creating a vacuum that pulls the lid down, sealing the jar. This vacuum seal is the guardian of the preserves, ensuring that the food remains safe and unspoiled.

The process begins with the selection of high-quality, high-acid ingredients. This selection is not merely a matter of taste but a critical safety consideration. High-acid foods naturally inhibit the growth of harmful bacteria, making them suitable for water bath canning. The journey of these ingredients, from garden to jar, is a celebration of the seasons, a way of capturing the essence of the harvest.

In preparing the food for canning, each step is an act of care. Fruits are washed, peeled, and chopped; tomatoes are blanched and peeled; herbs and spices are measured with precision. This preparation is a dialogue with the ingredients, a process where each piece is readied to become part of a greater whole.

The filling of the jars is a practice in mindfulness. The prepared food is packed into sterilized jars, leaving the appropriate headspace to allow for expansion during heating. This headspace, seemingly a small detail, is crucial in achieving a proper seal. The rims of the jars are wiped clean, ensuring that no residue interferes with the sealing process. Lids are placed on the jars, and the rings are tightened to fingertip tightness, a gentle yet firm securing of the lid.

The jars are then placed in a canner filled with water. The water bath, a gentle cradle, envelops the jars, ensuring that they are completely submerged. As the water comes to a boil, the dance of heat begins. The timing of the process, meticulously adhered to, varies depending on the type of food and the altitude. This timing is not arbitrary; it is a calculation that ensures the food is heated long enough to destroy any harmful microorganisms.

After the processing time, the jars are carefully removed from the water bath and left to cool. This cooling is not just a physical process but a transformation. As the jars cool, the lids make a distinctive pinging sound, a chorus that signals a successful seal. The jars are then stored, each one a testament to the art of preservation, a repository of flavors, and a symbol of self-sufficiency.

Step-by-Step Guide: Jams, Jellies, and Marmalades

Mango & Saffron Marmalade

- **P.T.:** 45 minutes
- **Acidity level:** High (added lemon juice)
- **Head Space:** 1/4 inch
- **Jar and Lid Preparation:** Sterilize jars and lids by boiling for 10 minutes.
- **Procedure:** In a pan, combine mango slices (peeled and diced), a pinch of saffron threads, equal parts sugar, and a splash of lemon juice. Bring to a boil, then simmer for 30 minutes until thickened. Pour into prepared jars.
- **Ingr.:** 4 ripe mangoes, peeled and diced; 1 pinch of saffron threads; 2 Cups sugar; 2 Tblsp lemon juice
- **Handling and Storage:** Store in a cool, dark place. Refrigerate after opening.

Spiced Blueberry Jam

- **P.T.:** 50 minutes
- **Acidity level:** Moderate
- **Head Space:** 1/4 inch
- **Jar and Lid Preparation:** Sterilize using boiling water method.
- **Procedure:** Mash fresh blueberries. In a pot, mix blueberries with sugar and a pinch of ground cardamom. Bring to a boil and continue boiling for 25 minutes, stirring frequently. Pour into jars.
- **Ingr.:** 3 Cups fresh blueberries, washed and mashed; 2 Cups sugar; 1/2 tsp ground cardamom.
- **Handling and Storage:** Cool, dark storage; refrigerate once opened.

Ginger-Pear Jelly

- **P.T.:** 1 hour
- **Acidity level:** High (pear and lemon juice)
- **Head Space:** 1/4 inch
- **Jar and Lid Preparation:** Sterilize in boiling water.
- **Procedure:** Combine pear juice, grated fresh ginger, sugar, and pectin in a large pot. Bring to a boil and continue boiling for 30 minutes. Pour into jars.

- **Ingr.:** 4 Cups pear juice; 2 Tblsp grated fresh ginger; 3 Cups sugar; 1 package pectin.
- **Handling and Storage:** Store in a cool, dark place; refrigerate after opening.

Raspberry-Lavender Jam

- **P.T.:** 1 hour
- **Acidity level:** Moderate
- **Head Space:** 1/4 inch
- **Jar Preparation:** Sterilize jars
- **Procedure:** Combine raspberries, dried lavender, sugar, and a squeeze of lemon juice in a pot. Bring to a boil and continue boiling for 35 minutes. Transfer to jars.

- **Ingr.:** 3 Cups fresh raspberries; 2 Cups sugar; 1 Tblsp dried lavender; 1 Tblsp lemon juice.
- **Handling and Storage:** Store in a cool, dark place; refrigerate after opening.

Blackberry-Chia Seed Jam

- **P.T.:** 45 minutes
- **Acidity level:** Moderate
- **Head Space:** 1/4 inch
- **Jar Preparation:** Sterilize through boiling.
- **Procedure:** Mash blackberries and mix with chia seeds, sugar, and a dash of lime juice. Cook over medium heat for 30 minutes. Ladle into jars.
- **Ingr.:** 3 Cups fresh blackberries, mashed; 2 Cups sugar; 1/4 Cups chia seeds, soaked in 1/2 Cups water; 1 Tblsp lime juice.
- **Handling and Storage:** Cool, dark storage; refrigerate once opened.

Apricot-Rosemary Jelly

- **P.T.:** 50 minutes
- **Acidity level:** High (apricot and lemon juice)
- **Head Space:** 1/4 inch
- **Jar Preparation:** Boil to sterilize.
- **Procedure:** In a pot, simmer apricot juice, a few rosemary sprigs, sugar, and pectin for 30 minutes. Pour into jars.
- **Ingr.:** 4 Cups apricot juice 2 Tblsp fresh rosemary sprigs; 3 Cups sugar; 1 package pectin.
- **Handling and Storage:** Store in a dark, cool place; refrigerate after opening.

Cherry-Almond Preserve

- **P.T.:** 1 hour
- **Acidity level:** Moderate
- **Head Space:** 1/4 inch
- **Jar Preparation:** Sterilize by boiling.
- **Procedure:** Combine pitted cherries, crushed almonds, sugar, and a few drops of almond extract in a pot. Bring to a boil and cook for 35 minutes. Transfer to jars.
- **Ingr.:** 3 Cups pitted cherries; 1/2 Cups crushed almonds; 2 Cups sugar; 1 tsp almond extract.
- **Handling and Storage:** Cool, dark storage; refrigerate once opened.

Orange-Cinnamon Marmalade

- **P.T.:** 1 hour
- **Acidity level:** High (orange and lemon juice)
- **Head Space:** 1/4 inch
- **Jar Preparation:** Boil to sterilize.
- **Procedure:** In a large pot, cook orange slices, cinnamon sticks, sugar, and a splash of lemon juice for 40 minutes. Pour into prepared jars.
- **Ingr.:** 4 Cups orange slices; 2 cinnamon sticks; 3 Cups sugar; 2 Tblsp lemon juice.
- **Handling and Storage:** Store in a cool, dark place; refrigerate after opening.

Strawberry-Basil Jam

- **P.T.:** 45 minutes
- **Acidity level:** Moderate
- **Head Space:** 1/4 inch
- **Jar Preparation:** Sterilize jars
- **Procedure:** Mash strawberries and combine with chopped fresh basil, sugar, and pectin in a pot. Bring to a boil and cook for 30 minutes. Ladle into jars.

- **Ingr.:** 4 Cups fresh strawberries, mashed; 2 Cups sugar; 1 package pectin; 1/4 Cups fresh basil, chopped.
- **Handling and Storage:** Store in a cool, dark place; refrigerate after opening.

Fig and Vanilla Bean Jam

- **P.T.:** 1 hour
- **Acidity level:** Moderate
- **Head Space:** 1/4 inch
- **Jar Preparation:** Sterilize in boiling water.
- **Procedure:** In a pot, simmer chopped figs, scraped vanilla beans, sugar, and lemon juice for 40 minutes. Pour into jars.

- **Ingr.:** 3 Cups fresh figs, chopped; 1 vanilla bean, split and scraped; 2 Cups sugar; 2 Tblsp lemon juice.
- **Handling and Storage:** Cool, dark storage; refrigerate once opened.

Pomegranate-Ginger Jelly

- **P.T.:** 50 minutes
- **Acidity level:** High (pomegranate juice and lemon)
- **Head Space:** 1/4 inch
- **Jar Preparation:** Sterilize through boiling for 10 minutes.
- **Procedure:** Mix pomegranate juice, grated fresh ginger, sugar, and lemon juice in a pot. Boil for 25 minutes, then pour into jars.
- **Ingr.:** 4 Cups pomegranate juice; 2 Tblsp grated fresh ginger; 3 Cups sugar; 2 Tblsp lemon juice.
- **Handling and Storage:** Store in a cool, dark place; refrigerate after opening.

Peach-Thyme Jam

- **P.T.:** 1 hour
- **Acidity level:** Moderate
- **Head Space:** 1/4 inch
- **Jar Preparation:** Sterilize by boiling.
- **Procedure:** Combine diced peaches, fresh thyme, sugar, and a dash of lemon juice in a pot. Boil for 35 minutes. Transfer to jars.
- **Ingr.:** 4 Cups peaches, diced; 2 Tblsp fresh thyme leaves; 3 Cups sugar; 2 Tblsp lemon juice.
- **Handling and Storage:** Store in a cool, dark place; refrigerate once opened.

Kiwi-Lime Preserve

- **P.T.:** 45 minutes
- **Acidity level:** High (lime juice)
- **Head Space:** 1/4 inch
- **Jar Preparation:** Boil to sterilize.
- **Procedure:** Slice kiwis and mix with sugar and lime juice in a pot. Boil for 30 minutes and ladle into jars.
- **Ingr.:** 4 Cups kiwi, peeled and sliced; 3 Cups sugar; 2 Tblsp lime juice.
- **Handling and Storage:** Cool, dark storage; refrigerate once opened.

Pineapple-Cilantro Jam

- **P.T.:** 50 minutes
- **Acidity level:** Moderate
- **Head Space:** 1/4 inch
- **Jar Preparation:** Sterilize jars
- **Procedure:** Mix chopped pineapple, cilantro leaves, sugar, and pineapple juice in a pot. Boil for 35 minutes and pour into jars.
- **Ingr.:** 3 Cups chopped pineapple; 1/4 Cups chopped cilantro; 2 Cups sugar; 1 Cup pineapple juice.
- **Handling and Storage:** Store in a cool, dark place; refrigerate after opening.

Plum-Star Anise Jam

- **P.T.:** 1 hour
- **Acidity level:** Moderate
- **Head Space:** 1/4 inch
- **Jar Preparation:** Sterilize in boiling water.
- **Procedure:** Halve plums and remove pits. Combine plums, sugar, star anise, and a splash of lemon juice in a pot. Cook for 40 minutes and jar.

- **Ingr.:** 4 Cups plums, halved and pitted; 3 Cups sugar; 2 star anise; 2 Tblsp lemon juice.
- **Handling and Storage:** Cool, dark storage; refrigerate once opened.

Grapefruit-Rose Jelly

- **P.T.:** 55 minutes
- **Acidity level:** High (grapefruit juice)
- **Head Space:** 1/4 inch
- **Jar Preparation:** Sterilize by boiling.
- **Procedure:** Combine grapefruit juice, dried rose petals, sugar, and pectin in a pot. Boil for 30 minutes. Ladle into jars.

- **Ingr.:** 4 Cups grapefruit juice; 2 Tblsp dried rose petals; 3 Cups sugar; 1 package pectin.
- **Handling and Storage:** Store in a cool, dark place; refrigerate after opening.

Apple-Cinnamon Butter

- **P.T.:** 1.5 hours
- **Acidity level:** Moderate
- **Head Space:** 1/4 inch
- **Jar Preparation:** Boil to sterilize.
- **Procedure:** Cook peeled, sliced apples with sugar, cinnamon sticks, and water. Simmer for 1 hour until thick. Remove cinnamon sticks and blend until smooth. Jar the mixture.
- **Ingr.:** 4 Cups apples, peeled and sliced; 2 Cups sugar; 2 cinnamon sticks; Cup water.
- **Handling and Storage:** Cool, dark storage; refrigerate once opened.

Red Currant-Chile Jelly

- **P.T.:** 50 minutes
- **Acidity level:** High (red currant juice)
- **Head Space:** 1/4 inch
- **Jar Preparation:** Sterilize jars
- **Procedure:** Mix red currant juice, finely chopped red chile, sugar, and pectin in a pot. Boil for 25 minutes. Pour into jars.
- **Ingr.:** 4 Cups red currant juice; 1 Tblsp finely chopped red chile; 3 Cups sugar; 1 package pectin.
- **Handling and Storage:** Store in a cool, dark place; refrigerate after opening.

Lemon-Basil Marmalade

- **P.T.:** 1 hour
- **Acidity level:** High (lemon juice)
- **Head Space:** 1/4 inch
- **Jar Preparation:** Sterilize through boiling.
- **Procedure:** Thinly slice lemons and combine with sugar, chopped basil, and water in a pot. Boil for 40 minutes, stirring frequently. Transfer to jars.
- **Ingr.:** 4 Cups lemons, thinly sliced; 3 Cups sugar; 1/4 Cups fresh basil, chopped; 1 Cup water.
- **Handling and Storage:** Cool, dark storage; refrigerate once opened.

Blackcurrant-Vanilla Jam

- **P.T.:** 1 hour
- **Acidity level:** Moderate
- **Head Space:** 1/4 inch
- **Jar Preparation:** Boil to sterilize.
- **Procedure:** Mix blackcurrants, sugar, scraped vanilla bean pods, and a little water in a pot. Boil for 35 minutes. Pour into jars.
- **Ingr.:** 3 Cups blackcurrants; 3 Cups sugar; 1 vanilla bean, split and scraped; 1/2 Cups water.
- **Handling and Storage:** Store in a cool, dark place; refrigerate after opening.

Preserving Fruits and Tomatoes: From Orchard to Jar

Spiced Peach Slices

- **P.T.:** 1 hour
- **Acidity level:** High (added lemon juice)
- **Head Space:** 1/2 inch
- **Jar Preparation:** Sterilize jars for 10 minutes in boiling water.
- **Procedure:** Combine peeled, sliced peaches with sugar, cinnamon, and a splash of lemon juice in a pot. Cook for 20 minutes, then ladle into jars.
- **Ingr.:** 4 Cups peaches, peeled and sliced; 2 Cups sugar; 1 tsp cinnamon; 2 Tblsp lemon juice.
- **Handling and Storage:** Store in a cool, dark place. Refrigerate after opening.

Tomato Basil Sauce

- **P.T.:** 1.5 hours
- **Acidity level:** High (tomatoes naturally and added lemon juice)
- **Head Space:** 1/2 inch
- **Jar Preparation:** Sterilize jars in boiling water.
- **Procedure:** Simmer crushed tomatoes, fresh basil, garlic, and lemon juice for 1 hour. Season and pour into jars.
- **Ingr.:** 4 Cups fresh tomatoes, crushed; 1/2 Cups fresh basil, chopped; 2 cloves garlic, minced; 2 Tblsp lemon juice.
- **Handling and Storage:** Store in a cool, dark place; refrigerate after opening.

Brandied Cherries

- **P.T.:** 1 hour
- **Acidity level:** Moderate
- **Head Space:** 1/2 inch
- **Jar Preparation:** Boil to sterilize.
- **Procedure:** Combine pitted cherries, brandy, sugar, and water in a pot. Cook for 15 minutes and transfer to jars.
- **Ingr.:** 4 Cups fresh cherries, pitted; 1 Cup brandy; 1 Cup sugar; 1 Cup water.
- **Handling and Storage:** Cool, dark storage; refrigerate once opened.

Honeyed Pear Preserves

- **P.T.:** 1 hour
- **Acidity level:** High (added lemon juice)
- **Head Space:** 1/2 inch
- **Jar Preparation:** Sterilize in boiling water.
- **Procedure:** Cook peeled, sliced pears with honey, a touch of cinnamon, and lemon juice for 30 minutes. Ladle into jars.
- **Ingr.:** 4 Cups pears, peeled and sliced; 1 Cup honey; 1/2 tsp cinnamon; 2 Tblsp lemon juice.
- **Handling and Storage:** Store in a cool, dark place; refrigerate after opening.

Apple Cider Compote

- **P.T.:** 1 hour
- **Acidity level:** Moderate
- **Head Space:** 1/2 inch
- **Jar Preparation:** Sterilize jars
- **Procedure:** Simmer diced apples in apple cider with a pinch of nutmeg for 25 minutes. Transfer to jars.
- **Ingr.:** 4 Cups apples, diced; 2 Cups apple cider; 1/2 tsp nutmeg.
- **Handling and Storage:** Store in a cool, dark place; refrigerate after opening.

Lemon-Preserved Figs

- **P.T.:** 50 minutes
- **Acidity level:** High (lemon syrup)
- **Head Space:** 1/2 inch
- **Jar Preparation:** Boil to sterilize.
- **Procedure:** Simmer whole figs in a lemon juice and sugar syrup for 20 minutes. Pour into jars.
- **Ingr.:** 4 Cups whole figs; 2 Cups sugar; 1 Cup lemon juice.
- **Handling and Storage:** Cool, dark storage; refrigerate once opened.

Zesty Orange Marmalade

- **P.T.:** 1.5 hours
- **Acidity level:** High (natural and added lemon juice)
- **Head Space:** 1/4 inch
- **Jar Preparation:** Sterilize by boiling.
- **Procedure:** Cook thinly sliced oranges with sugar and lemon juice for 1 hour. Jar the mixture.
- **Ingr.:** 4 Cups oranges, thinly sliced; 3 Cups sugar; 2 Tblsp lemon juice.
- **Handling and Storage:** Store in a cool, dark place; refrigerate after opening.

Spicy Tomato Chutney

- **P.T.:** 1 hour
- **Acidity level:** High (tomatoes and vinegar)
- **Head Space:** 1/2 inch
- **Jar Preparation:** Sterilize through boiling.
- **Procedure:** Cook diced tomatoes, apple cider vinegar, brown sugar, and spices for 45 minutes. Ladle into jars.
- **Ingr.:** 4 Cups tomatoes, diced; 1 Cup apple cider vinegar; 1 Cup brown sugar; 1 Tblsp mixed spices.
- **Handling and Storage:** Cool, dark storage; refrigerate once opened.

Vanilla-Infused Plums

- **P.T.:** 1 hour
- **Acidity level:** Moderate
- **Head Space:** 1/2 inch
- **Jar Preparation:** Sterilize jars
- **Procedure:** Halve plums and remove pits. Simmer in a vanilla and sugar syrup for 25 minutes. Transfer to jars.

- **Ingr.:** 4 Cups plums, halved and pitted; 2 Cups sugar; 1 vanilla pod, split.
- **Handling and Storage:** Store in a cool, dark place; refrigerate after opening.

Rustic Grape Jam

- **P.T.:** 1 hour
- **Acidity level:** Moderate
- **Head Space:** 1/4 inch
- **Jar Preparation:** Sterilize in boiling water.
- **Procedure:** Mash grapes, cook with sugar and a squeeze of lemon juice for 35 minutes. Pour into jars.

- **Ingr.:** 4 Cups grapes, mashed; 2 Cups sugar; 2 Tblsp lemon juice.
- **Handling and Storage:** Cool, dark storage; refrigerate once opened.

Cinnamon-Spiced Applesauce

- **P.T.:** 1.5 hours
- **Acidity level:** High (natural and added lemon juice)
- **Head Space:** 1/2 inch
- **Jar Preparation:** Sterilize by boiling.
- **Procedure:** Cook peeled, diced apples with cinnamon, sugar, and lemon juice for 1 hour. Blend to desired consistency and jar.

- **Ingr.:** 4 Cups apples, peeled and diced; 1 tsp cinnamon; 2 Cups sugar; 2 Tblsp lemon juice.
- **Handling and Storage:** Store in a cool, dark place; refrigerate after opening.

Sweet Cherry Preserve

- **P.T.:** 1 hour
- **Acidity level:** Moderate
- **Head Space:** 1/2 inch
- **Jar Preparation:** Sterilize through boiling.
- **Procedure:** Pit cherries and cook with sugar and a dash of almond extract for 30 minutes. Transfer to jars.

- **Ingr.:** 4 Cups cherries, pitted; 2 Cups sugar; 1 tsp almond extract.
- **Handling and Storage:** Cool, dark storage; refrigerate once opened.

Fiery Peppered Tomato Relish

- **P.T.:** 1 hour
- **Acidity level:** High (tomatoes and vinegar)
- **Head Space:** 1/2 inch
- **Jar Preparation:** Sterilize jars
- **Procedure:** Simmer diced tomatoes, bell peppers, hot peppers, vinegar, and sugar for 45 minutes. Pour into jars
- **Ingr.:** 4 Cups tomatoes, diced; 1 Cup bell peppers, diced; 1/2 Cups hot peppers, diced; 1 Cup vinegar; 1 Cup sugar.
- **Handling and Storage:** Store in a cool, dark place; refrigerate after opening.

Mulled Wine Grapes

- **P.T.:** 1 hour
- **Acidity level:** Moderate
- **Head Space:** 1/2 inch
- **Jar Preparation:** Sterilize in boiling water.
- **Procedure:** Simmer whole grapes in a mulled wine mixture for 30 minutes. Ladle into jars.
- **Ingr.:** 4 Cups whole grapes; 2 Cups mulled wine mixture.
- **Handling and Storage:** Cool, dark storage; refrigerate once opened.

Gingered Pear Chutney

- **P.T.:** 1 hour
- **Acidity level:** High (pear and lemon juice)
- **Head Space:** 1/2 inch
- **Jar Preparation:** Boil to sterilize.
- **Procedure:** Cook diced pears with fresh ginger, sugar, vinegar, and spices for 40 minutes. Pour into jars.
- **Ingr.:** 4 Cups pears, diced; 2 Tblsp fresh ginger, grated; 2 Cups sugar; 1 Cup vinegar; 1 Tblsp mixed spices.
- **Handling and Storage:** Store in a cool, dark place; refrigerate after opening.

Balsamic Strawberry Compote

- **P.T.:** 1 hour
- **Acidity level:** Moderate
- **Head Space:** 1/2 inch
- **Jar Preparation:** Sterilize by boiling.
- **Procedure:** Combine halved strawberries with balsamic vinegar, sugar, and a pinch of black pepper. Cook for 30 minutes. Transfer to jars.
- **Ingr.:** 4 Cups strawberries, halved; 1 Cup balsamic vinegar; 1 Cup sugar; 1/2 tsp black pepper.
- **Handling and Storage:** Cool, dark storage; refrigerate once opened.

Lemony Fig Spread

- **P.T.:** 1 hour
- **Acidity level:** High (figs and lemon juice)
- **Head Space:** 1/2 inch
- **Jar Preparation:** Sterilize through boiling.
- **Procedure:** Simmer chopped figs with lemon juice, sugar, and water for 35 minutes. Ladle into jars.
- **Ingr.:** 4 Cups figs, chopped; 1 Cup lemon juice; 2 Cups sugar; 1 Cup water.
- **Handling and Storage:** Store in a cool, dark place; refrigerate after opening.

Vanilla Bean Peaches

- **P.T.:** 1 hour 30 minutes
- **Acidity level:** High (with added lemon juice)
- **Head Space:** 1/2 inch
- **Jar Preparation:** Sterilize jars by boiling for 10 minutes.
- **Procedure:** Peel and slice peaches. In a pot, simmer with water, sugar, and vanilla bean for 20 minutes. Add lemon juice, then pack into jars and process in water bath for 25 minutes.
- **Ingr.:** 4 Cups peaches, peeled and sliced; 2 Cups water; 2 Cups sugar; 1 vanilla bean, split; 2 Tblsp lemon juice.
- **Handling and Storage:** Store in a cool, dark place. Refrigerate after opening.

Spicy Tomato Salsa

- **P.T.:** 1 hour
- **Acidity level:** High (tomatoes and vinegar)
- **Head Space:** 1/2 inch
- **Jar Preparation:** Sterilize through boiling.
- **Procedure:** Combine chopped tomatoes, onions, jalapeños, cilantro, vinegar, and spices. Simmer for 10 minutes. Fill jars and process in water bath for 15 minutes.
- **Ingr.:** 4 Cups tomatoes, chopped; 1 Cup onions, chopped; 1/2 Cups jalapeños, chopped; 1/4 Cups cilantro, finely chopped; 1 Cup vinegar; 1 Tblsp mixed spices.
- **Handling and Storage:** Keep in a cool, dark place; refrigerate after opening.

Bourbon-Infused Cherries

- **P.T.:** 1 hour
- **Acidity level:** High (with added lemon juice)
- **Head Space:** 1/2 inch
- **Jar Preparation:** Sterilize in boiling water.
- **Procedure:** Pit cherries and pack into jars. In a pot, heat bourbon, sugar, and lemon juice until sugar dissolves. Pour over cherries and process in water bath for 25 minutes.
- **Ingr.:** 4 Cups cherries, pitted; 1 Cup bourbon; 1 Cup sugar; 2 Tblsp lemon juice.
- **Handling and Storage:** Store jars in a cool, dark place. Refrigerate after opening.

Acidic Foods Canning: Pickles, Relishes, and Chutneys

Spiced Cauliflower Pickles

- **P.T.:** 1 hour 20 minutes
- **Acidity level:** High (with vinegar)
- **Head Space:** 1/2 inch
- **Jar Preparation:** Sterilize jars by boiling for 10 minutes.
- **Procedure:** Blanch cauliflower florets for 3 minutes. In a pot, boil vinegar, water, sugar, and spices for 5 minutes. Add cauliflower and simmer for 2 minutes. Pack into jars and process in a water bath for 10 minutes.
- **Ingr.:** 4 Cups cauliflower florets; 2 Cups vinegar; 1 Cup water; 1 Cup sugar; 2 Tblsp spice mix.
- **Handling and Storage:** Store in a cool, dark place. Refrigerate after opening.

Mango-Lime Chutney

- **P.T.:** 1 hour
- **Acidity level:** High (with lime juice and vinegar)
- **Head Space:** 1/2 inch
- **Jar Preparation:** Sterilize through boiling.
- **Procedure:** Combine chopped mango, lime juice, vinegar, sugar, and spices in a pot. Simmer for 45 minutes. Pour into jars and process in a water bath for 15 minutes.
- **Ingr.:** 4 Cups mango, peeled and chopped; 2 Tblsp lime juice; 1 Cup vinegar; 2 Cups sugar; 1 Tblsp spice mix.
- **Handling and Storage:** Keep in a cool, dark place; refrigerate after opening.

Dill Garlic Cucumbers

- **P.T.:** 1 hour 30 minutes
- **Acidity level:** High (with vinegar)
- **Head Space:** 1/2 inch
- **Jar Preparation:** Sterilize in boiling water.
- **Procedure:** Slice cucumbers. In a pot, boil vinegar, water, and salt for 5 minutes. Add cucumbers, garlic, and dill. Simmer for 5 minutes. Pack into jars and process in a water bath for 10 minutes.
- **Ingr.:** 4 Cups cucumbers, sliced; 2 Cups vinegar; 2 Cups water; 1 Tblsp salt; 2 cloves garlic; 2 Tblsp dill.
- **Handling and Storage:** Store jars in a cool, dark place. Refrigerate after opening.

Carrot and Ginger Relish

- **P.T.:** 45 minutes
- **Acidity level:** High (with vinegar)
- **Head Space:** 1/2 inch
- **Jar Preparation:** Boil to sterilize.
- **Procedure:** Grate carrots and ginger. In a pot, mix vinegar, sugar, and spices. Add carrots and ginger, cook for 10 minutes. Fill jars and process in water bath for 15 minutes.
- **Ingr.:** 4 Cups carrots, peeled and grated; 2 Tblsp fresh ginger, grated; 2 Cups vinegar; 2 Cups sugar; 1 Tblsp spice mix.
- **Handling and Storage:** Cool, dark storage; refrigerate once opened.

Sweet and Spicy Zucchini Pickles

- **P.T.:** 1 hour
- **Acidity level:** High (with vinegar)
- **Head Space:** 1/2 inch
- **Jar Preparation:** Sterilize jars
- **Procedure:** Slice zucchini. Boil vinegar, sugar, and spices for 5 minutes. Add zucchini and simmer for 2 minutes. Pack into jars and process in a water bath for 10 minutes.
- **Ingr.:** 4 Cups zucchini, sliced; 2 Cups vinegar; 1 Cup sugar; 2 Tblsp spice mix.
- **Handling and Storage:** Store in a cool, dark place; refrigerate after opening.

Green Tomato Chutney

- **P.T.:** 1 hour 15 minutes
- **Acidity level:** High (with vinegar)
- **Head Space:** 1/2 inch
- **Jar Preparation:** Boil to sterilize.
- **Procedure:** Chop green tomatoes. In a pot, simmer tomatoes, onions, sugar, vinegar, and spices for 1 hour. Pour into jars and process in a water bath for 15 minutes.
- **Ingr.:** 4 Cups green tomatoes, chopped; 1 Cup onions, chopped; 2 Cups sugar; 1 Cup vinegar; 1 Tblsp spice mix.
- **Handling and Storage:** Cool, dark storage; refrigerate once opened.

Hot Jalapeño Relish

- **P.T.:** 50 minutes
- **Acidity level:** High (with vinegar)
- **Head Space:** 1/2 inch
- **Jar Preparation:** Sterilize through boiling.
- **Procedure:** Finely chop jalapeños and onions. Cook with vinegar, sugar, and salt for 20 minutes. Fill jars and process in a water bath for 15 minutes.
- **Ingr.:** 4 Cups jalapeños, finely chopped; 1 Cup onions, finely chopped; 2 Cups vinegar; 1 Cup sugar; 1 Tblsp salt.
- **Handling and Storage:** Store in a cool, dark place; refrigerate after opening.

Red Onion Marmalade

- **P.T.:** 1 hour
- **Acidity level:** High (with balsamic vinegar)
- **Head Space:** 1/2 inch
- **Jar Preparation:** Sterilize jars
- **Procedure:** Thinly slice red onions. In a pot, simmer onions with balsamic vinegar, sugar, and a pinch of salt for 45 minutes. Pack into jars and process in a water bath for 15 minutes.
- **Ingr.:** 4 Cups red onions, thinly sliced; 2 Cups balsamic vinegar; 1 Cup sugar; 1 tsp salt.
- **Handling and Storage:** Store in a cool, dark place; refrigerate after opening.

Bell Pepper and Apple Chutney

- **P.T.:** 1 hour 20 minutes
- **Acidity level:** High (with vinegar and lemon juice)
- **Head Space:** 1/2 inch
- **Jar Preparation:** Sterilize in boiling water.
- **Procedure:** Chop bell peppers and apples. Cook with vinegar, sugar, lemon juice, and spices for 1 hour. Pour into jars and process in a water bath for 15 minutes.
- **Ingr.:** 2 Cups bell peppers, chopped; 2 Cups apples, chopped; 1 Cup vinegar; 2 Cups sugar; 2 Tblsp lemon juice; 1 Tblsp spice mix.
- **Handling and Storage:** Cool, dark storage; refrigerate once opened.

Classic Bread and Butter Pickles

- **P.T.:** 1 hour 30 minutes
- **Acidity level:** High (with vinegar)
- **Head Space:** 1/2 inch
- **Jar Preparation:** Sterilize jars and lids.
- **Procedure:** Slice cucumbers and onions. Soak in salted ice water for 2 hours. Drain and rinse. In a pot, boil vinegar, sugar, and spices. Add cucumbers and onions, simmer for 5 minutes. Pack into jars and process in a water bath for 10 minutes.
- **Ingr.:** 4 Cups cucumbers, sliced; 1 Cup onions, sliced; 2 Cups vinegar; 2 Cups sugar; 1 Tblsp spice mix.
- **Handling and Storage:** Store in a cool, dark place; refrigerate after opening.

Cranberry-Orange Relish

- **P.T.:** 50 minutes
- **Acidity level:** High (with orange juice)
- **Head Space:** 1/2 inch
- **Jar Preparation:** Sterilize through boiling.
- **Procedure:** Combine cranberries, orange zest, and orange juice in a pot. Add sugar and cook for 30 minutes. Ladle into jars an process in a water bath for 15 minutes.
- **Ingr.:** 4 Cups cranberries; 2 Tblsp orange zest; 1 Cup orange juice; 2 Cups sugar
- **Handling and Storage:** Store in a cool, dark place; refrigerate after opening.

Spicy Corn Relish

- **P.T.:** 1 hour 10 minutes
- **Acidity level:** High (with vinegar)
- **Head Space:** 1/2 inch
- **Jar Preparation:** Sterilize in boiling water.
- **Procedure:** Sauté corn kernels, bell peppers, and onions. Add vinegar, sugar, and spices, and simmer for 20 minutes. Fill jars and process in a water bath for 15 minutes.
- **Ingr.:** 2 Cups corn kernels 1 Cup bell peppers, chopped; 1 Cup onions, chopped; 2 Cups vinegar; Cup sugar; 1 Tblsp spice mix.
- **Handling and Storage:** Cool, dark storage; refrigerate once opened.

Pear and Ginger Chutney

- **P.T.:** 1 hour
- **Acidity level:** High (with lemon juice)
- **Head Space:** 1/2 inch
- **Jar Preparation:** Boil to sterilize.
- **Procedure:** Chop pears and mix with grated ginger, lemon juice, sugar, and spices.

Cook for 40 minutes. Pour into jars and process in a water bath for 15 minutes.

- **Ingr.:** 4 Cups pears, peeled and chopped; 2 Tblsp fresh ginger, grated; 2 Tblsp lemon juice; 2 Cups sugar; 1 Tblsp spice mix.
- **Handling and Storage:** Store in a cool, dark place; refrigerate after opening.

Beetroot and Onion Pickle

- **P.T.:** 1 hour 30 minutes
- **Acidity level:** High (with vinegar)
- **Head Space:** 1/2 inch
- **Jar Preparation:** Sterilize jars
- **Procedure:** Boil beetroot until tender. Sauté onions, then add cooked beetroot, vinegar, sugar, and spices.

Simmer for 20 minutes. Ladle into jars and process in a water bath for 10 minutes.

- **Ingr.:** 4 Cups beetroot, boiled and peeled; 1 Cup onions, sliced; 2 Cups vinegar; 1 Cup sugar; 1 Tblsp spice mix.
- **Handling and Storage:** Cool, dark storage; refrigerate once opened.

Cucumber and Mint Chutney

- **P.T.:** 45 minutes
- **Acidity level:** High (with lemon juice)
- **Head Space:** 1/2 inch
- **Jar Preparation:** Sterilize through boiling.
- **Procedure:** Blend cucumbers, mint leaves, green chilies, lemon juice, and sugar. Cook for 15 minutes. Pack into jars and process in a water bath for 10 minutes.
- **Ingr.:** 4 Cups cucumbers, chopped; 1 Cup mint leaves; 2 green chilies; 2 Tblsp lemon juice; 1 Cup sugar.
- **Handling and Storage:** Store in a cool, dark place; refrigerate after opening.

Garlic Dill Green Beans

- **P.T.:** 1 hour
- **Acidity level:** High (with vinegar)
- **Head Space:** 1/2 inch
- **Jar Preparation:** Sterilize in boiling water.
- **Procedure:** Pack trimmed green beans, dill, and garlic into jars. Boil vinegar, water, and salt, then pour over beans. Process in a water bath for 10 minutes.
- **Ingr.:** 4 Cups green beans, trimmed; 2 cloves garlic; 2 Tblsp dill; 2 Cups vinegar; 2 Cups water; 1 Tblsp salt.
- **Handling and Storage:** Cool, dark storage; refrigerate once opened.

Apple-Cider Vinegar Onions

- **P.T.:** 1 hour 20 minutes
- **Acidity level:** High (with apple cider vinegar)
- **Head Space:** 1/2 inch
- **Jar Preparation:** Sterilize jars
- **Procedure:** Slice onions and pack into jars. Heat apple cider vinegar, water, and sugar, then pour over onions. Process in a water bath for 15 minutes.
- **Ingr.:** 4 Cups onions, thinly sliced; 2 Cups apple cider vinegar; 1 Cup water; 1 Cup sugar.
- **Handling and Storage:** Store in a cool, dark place; refrigerate after opening.

Lemon and Rosemary Olives

- **P.T.:** 45 minutes
- **Acidity level:** High (with lemon juice)
- **Head Space:** 1/2 inch
- **Jar Preparation:** Boil to sterilize.
- **Procedure:** Mix olives, lemon slices, rosemary, and olive oil. Add lemon juice and vinegar, and simmer for 10 minutes. Pack into jars and process in a water bath for 10 minutes.
- **Ingr.:** 4 Cups olives; 2 lemons, sliced; 2 Tblsp rosemary; 1/4 Cups olive oil; 1 Cup vinegar; 1 Cup lemon juice.
- **Handling and Storage:** Store in a cool, dark place; refrigerate after opening.

Sweet Pepper Jam

- **P.T.:** 1 hour
- **Acidity level:** High (with vinegar)
- **Head Space:** 1/2 inch
- **Jar Preparation:** Sterilize through boiling.
- **Procedure:** Chop bell peppers and mix with sugar, vinegar, and pectin. Boil for 30 minutes. Ladle into jars and process in a water bath for 15 minutes.
- **Ingr.:** 4 Cups bell peppers chopped; 3 Cups sugar; 1 Cup vinegar; 1 package pectin.
- **Handling and Storage:** Store in a cool, dark place; refrigerate after opening.

Tamarind Date Chutney

- **P.T.:** 1 hour 10 minutes
- **Acidity level:** High (with tamarind)
- **Head Space:** 1/2 inch
- **Jar Preparation:** Sterilize in boiling water.
- **Procedure:** Soak tamarind and dates in water. Blend into a puree. Cook with sugar, spices, and vinegar for 40 minutes. Pour into jars and process in a water bath for 15 minutes.
- **Ingr.:** 1 Cup tamarind, soaked; 1 Cup dates, soaked; 2 Cups sugar; 1 Tblsp spice mix; 1 Cup vinegar.
- **Handling and Storage:** Cool, dark storage; refrigerate once opened.

Book III: Pressure Canning

Understanding Pressure Canning: The Science and Method

Pressure canning, at its core, is a method that employs high-temperature steam under pressure to preserve food in airtight containers. This technique is particularly essential for low-acid foods such as vegetables, meats, poultry, and seafood, which are not suitable for water bath canning due to their pH levels. These foods require temperatures beyond the boiling point of water to effectively destroy potentially harmful microorganisms like Clostridium botulinum, the bacteria responsible for botulism. Pressure canning achieves this by elevating the boiling point of water, thereby allowing food to reach temperatures above 240°F (116°C), a realm where these stubborn microorganisms cannot survive.

The science behind pressure canning is both profound and simple. At the heart of this method is the principle of steam pressure. As water boils, it creates steam, which builds up pressure within the sealed environment of a pressure canner. This increased pressure raises the boiling point of water, allowing the contents of the jars to be heated to a much higher temperature than would be possible in a regular boiling water bath. It is this elevated temperature, uniformly distributed throughout the canner, that ensures the thorough sterilization of the food.

But understanding pressure canning is not just about comprehending the science; it is also about recognizing the method's intricacies. The process begins with the meticulous preparation of the food and canning jars. Foods are prepared according to tested recipes, ensuring that they are of the highest quality and free from any contaminants. Jars are carefully cleaned and inspected for any flaws that could compromise the integrity of the seal.

Once the food is prepared and packed into jars, the art of pressure canning begins. The jars are placed into the pressure canner, a sturdy vessel designed to withstand high pressure. Water is added, but unlike in water bath canning, it does not cover the jars. Instead, it is the steam generated from this water that will envelop the jar and cook the contents. The canner lid, equipped with a vent, a pressure gauge, and safety valve, is securely locked in place, creating an airtight seal.

As the water boils and steam begins to fill the canner, a crucial step is the venting of air. This process, known as "exhausting," involves allowing steam to flow freely from the vent for a specific period. This step is vital as it ensures the removal of air from the canner, allowing the steam to evenly and effectively heat the contents of the jars. Once the canner is adequately vented, the weight or pressure regulator is placed on the vent, and the pressure begins to build. The canner's gauge allows for careful monitoring as the pressure rises to the required level for the specific type of food being processed. This stage requires vigilant attention, as maintaining the correct pressure is critical for safety and effectiveness. The processing time, determined by tested recipes and adjusted for altitude, begins once the desired pressure is reached. After the processing time is complete, the canner is removed from heat, and the pressure is allowed to drop naturally. This gradual decrease in pressure is as critical as the rise, ensuring the safety of the jars and the quality of the food inside. Once the pressure returns to normal, the lid is removed, and the jars are carefully taken out and left to cool. The cooling process is not just a conclusion but a continuation of the science, as the contents of the jars contract, creating a vacuum seal that locks in freshness and safety.

Canning Vegetables and Soups: A Comprehensive Guide

Hearty Vegetable Soup

- **P.T.:** 2 hours
- **Acidity level:** Adjusted with lemon juice
- **Head Space:** 1 inch
- **Jar Preparation:** Sterilize jars
- **Procedure:** Sauté a mix of diced carrots, potatoes, celery, and onions. Add vegetable broth and seasonings. Simmer for 1 hour. Process in pressure canner for 75 minutes at 11 psi.
- **Ingr.:** 2 Cups carrots, peeled and diced; 2 Cups potatoes, peeled and diced; 1 Cup celery, diced; 1 Cup onions, diced; 6 Cups vegetable broth; 1 Tblsp lemon juice.
- **Handling and Storage:** Store in a cool, dark place. Use within a year.

Classic Beef Stew

- **P.T.:** 2.5 hours
- **Acidity level:** Low; pressure canning required
- **Head Space:** 1 inch
- **Jar Preparation:** Sterilize jars
- **Procedure:** Brown cubed beef and transfer to a pot. Add diced potatoes, carrots, onions, beef broth, and seasonings. Simmer for 1 hour. Fill jars and process at 11 psi for 90 minutes.
- **Ingr.:** 2 lb. beef, cubed; 2 Cups potatoes, peeled and diced; 1 Cup carrots, peeled and diced; 1 Cup onions, diced; 6 Cups beef broth.

- **Handling and Storage:**

  Store in a cool, dark place.

  Consume within a year.

Spiced Carrot Soup

- **P.T.:** 1 hour 30 minutes
- **Acidity level:** Adjusted with lemon juice
- **Head Space:** 1 inch
- **Jar Preparation:** Sterilize jars
- **Procedure:** Cook diced carrots, onions, ginger, and spices until soft. Blend into a puree.

  Process in pressure canner for 55 minutes at 11 psi.
- **Ingr.:** 4 Cups carrots, peeled and diced; 1 Cup onions, chopped; 2 Tblsp ginger, peeled and diced; 1 tsp mixed spices; 1 Tblsp lemon juice.
- **Handling and Storage:** Store in a cool, dark place. Use within one year.

Chicken Noodle Soup

- **P.T.:** 2 hours
- **Acidity level:** Low; pressure canning required
- **Head Space:** 1 inch
- **Jar Preparation:** Sterilize jars
- **Procedure:** Cook chicken, carrots, celery, onions in broth. Add noodles. Cook until tender.

  Process in pressure canner for 75 minutes at 11 psi.
- **Ingr.:** 2 lb. chicken, cubed; 1 Cup carrots, diced; 1 Cup celery, diced; 1 Cup onions, diced; 6 Cups chicken broth; 2 Cups noodles.
- **Handling and Storage:** Store in a cool, dark place. Use within a year.

Tomato Basil Soup

- **P.T.:** 1 hour 30 minutes
- **Acidity level:** Adjusted with lemon juice
- **Head Space:** 1 inch
- **Jar Preparation:** Sterilize jars
- **Procedure:** Cook tomatoes, onions, garlic, and basil. Puree and return to pot. Add broth. Process in pressure canner for 55 minutes at 11 psi.
- **Ingr.:** 4 Cups tomatoes, chopped; 1 Cup onions, chopped; 2 cloves garlic, minced; 1/4 Cups basil, chopped; 4 Cups vegetable broth; 1 Tblsp lemon juice.
- **Handling and Storage:** Store in a cool, dark place. Use within a year.

Lentil Soup with Vegetables

- **P.T.:** 2 hours
- **Acidity level:** Low; pressure canning required
- **Head Space:** 1 inch
- **Jar Preparation:** Sterilize jars
- **Procedure:** Sauté onions, carrots, and celery. Add lentils, broth, and spices. Simmer until lentils are tender. Process in pressure canner for 75 minutes at 11 psi.
- **Ingr.:** 2 Cups lentils, rinsed; 1 Cup onions, chopped; 1 Cup carrots, diced; 1 Cup celery, diced; 6 Cups vegetable broth.
- **Handling and Storage:** Store in a cool, dark place. Consume within a year.

Split Pea and Ham Soup

- **P.T.:** 2 hours 30 minutes
- **Acidity level:** Low; pressure canning required
- **Head Space:** 1 inch
- **Jar Preparation:** Sterilize jars
- **Procedure:** Cook split peas, diced ham, carrots, onions, and broth until peas are soft. Process in pressure canner for 90 minutes at 11 psi.
- **Ingr.:** 2 Cups split peas, rinsed; 1 lb. ham, diced; 1 Cup carrots, diced; 1 Cup onions, diced; 6 Cups chicken broth.
- **Handling and Storage:** Store in a cool, dark place. Use within a year.

Creamy Potato Soup

- **P.T.:** 2 hours
- **Acidity level:** Low; pressure canning required
- **Head Space:** 1 inch
- **Jar Preparation:** Sterilize jars
- **Procedure:** Cook diced potatoes, onions, celery in broth. Blend some potatoes for thickness. Process in pressure canner for 75 minutes at 11 psi.
- **Ingr.:** 4 Cups potatoes, peeled and diced; 1 Cup onions, chopped; 1 Cup celery, diced; 6 Cups chicken broth.
- **Handling and Storage:** Store in a cool, dark place. Consume within a year.

Vegetable Minestrone

- **P.T.:** 2 hours
- **Acidity level:** Low; pressure canning required
- **Head Space:** 1 inch
- **Jar Preparation:** Sterilize jars
- **Procedure:** Cook a mix of vegetables, beans, tomatoes, pasta, and broth. Simmer until vegetables are tender. Process in pressure canner for 75 minutes at 11 psi.
- **Ingr.:** 2 Cups mixed vegetables, diced; 1 Cup beans, cooked; 1 Cup tomatoes, chopped; 1/2 Cups pasta; 6 Cups vegetable broth.
- **Handling and Storage:** Store in a cool, dark place. Use within a year.

Corn and Chicken Chowder

- **P.T.:** 2 hours
- **Acidity level:** Low; pressure canning required
- **Head Space:** 1 inch
- **Jar Preparation:** Sterilize jars
- **Procedure:** Sauté chicken, corn, potatoes, onions, and peppers. Add broth and cream. Cook until thick. Process in pressure canner for 90 minutes at 11 psi.
- **Ingr.:** 1 lb. chicken, cubed; 2 Cups corn; 2 Cups potatoes, diced; 1 Cup onions, chopped; 1 Cup peppers, diced; 6 Cups chicken broth; 1 Cup cream.
- **Handling and Storage:** Store in a cool, dark place. Consume within a year

Rustic Beef Barley Soup

- **P.T.:** 2 hours 30 minutes
- **Acidity level:** Low; pressure canning required
- **Head Space:** 1 inch
- **Jar Preparation:** Sterilize jars
- **Procedure:** Brown cubed beef; add barley, diced carrots, celery, onions, and beef broth. Simmer until barley is tender. Process in pressure canner for 90 minutes at 11 psi.
- **Ingr.:** 2 lb. beef, cubed; 1 Cup barley, rinsed; 1 Cup carrots, diced; 1 Cup celery, diced; 1 Cup onions, diced; 6 Cups beef broth.
- **Handling and Storage:** Store in a cool, dark place. Consume within a year.

Chunky Vegetable Broth

- **P.T.:** 2 hours
- **Acidity level:** Adjusted with lemon juice
- **Head Space:** 1 inch
- **Jar and Lid Preparation:** Sterilize jars and lids.
- **Procedure:** Combine various chopped vegetables, herbs, water, and a splash of lemon juice. Simmer for 1 hour. Strain and process the liquid in pressure canner for 75 minutes at 11 psi.
- **Ingr.:** 4 Cups mixed vegetables, chopped; 1/4 Cups fresh herbs; 6 Cups water; 1 Tblsp lemon juice.
- **Handling and Storage:** Store in a cool, dark place. Use within a year.

Curried Lentil Soup

- **P.T.:** 2 hours
- **Acidity level:** Low; pressure canning required
- **Head Space:** 1 inch
- **Jar and Lid Preparation:** Sterilize jars and lids.
- **Procedure:** Cook lentils, diced tomatoes, onions, and curry spices in vegetable broth until lentils are soft. Process in pressure canner for 75 minutes at 11 psi.
- **Ingr.:** 2 Cups lentils, rinsed; 1 Cup tomatoes, diced; 1 Cup onions, diced; 1 Tblsp curry spices; 6 Cups vegetable broth.
- **Handling and Storage:** Store in a cool, dark place. Consume within a year.

Italian Minestrone with Pasta

- **P.T.:** 2 hours 30 minutes
- **Acidity level:** Low; pressure canning required
- **Head Space:** 1 inch
- **Jar and Lid Preparation:** Sterilize jars and lids.
- **Procedure:** Sauté onions, garlic, carrots, and celery. Add tomatoes, beans, pasta, and herbs. Cook until pasta is al dente. Process in pressure canner for 90 minutes at 11 psi.
- **Ingr.:** 1 Cup onions, chopped; 2 cloves garlic, minced; 1 Cup carrots, diced; 1 Cup celery, diced; 1 Cup tomatoes, chopped; 1 Cup beans, cooked; 1/2 Cups pasta; 1 Tblsp Italian herbs.
- **Handling and Storage:** Store in a cool, dark place. Use within a year.

Savory Mushroom Soup

- **P.T.:** 1 hour 45 minutes
- **Acidity level:** Low; pressure canning required
- **Head Space:** 1 inch
- **Jar and Lid Preparation:** Sterilize jars and lids.
- **Procedure:** Sauté assorted mushrooms with onions and garlic. Add vegetable broth and seasonings. Simmer for 30 minutes. Process in pressure canner for 75 minutes at 11 psi.
- **Ingr.:** 4 Cups mushrooms, sliced; 1 Cup onions, chopped; 2 cloves garlic, minced; 6 Cups vegetable broth.
- **Handling and Storage:** Store in a cool, dark place. Consume within a year.

Spicy Black Bean Soup

- **P.T.:** 2 hours
- **Acidity level:** Low; pressure canning required
- **Head Space:** 1 inch
- **Jar and Lid Preparation:** Sterilize jars and lids.
- **Procedure:** Cook soaked black beans with onions, peppers, and spices in chicken broth. Puree some beans for thickness. Process in pressure canner for 75 minutes at 11 psi.
- **Ingr.:** 2 Cups black beans, soaked; 1 Cup onions, diced; 1 Cup peppers, diced; 1 Tblsp spice mix; 6 Cups chicken broth.
- **Handling and Storage:** Store in a cool, dark place. Consume within a year.

Cream of Asparagus Soup

- **P.T.:** 2 hours
- **Acidity level:** Low; pressure canning required
- **Head Space:** 1 inch
- **Jar and Lid Preparation:** Sterilize jars and lids.
- **Procedure:** Cook chopped asparagus with onions in chicken broth. Blend into a puree. Process in pressure canner for 75 minutes at 11 psi.
- **Ingr.:** 4 Cups asparagus, chopped; 1 Cup onions, diced; 6 Cups chicken broth.
- **Handling and Storage:** Store in a cool, dark place. Use within a year.

Potato Leek Soup

- **P.T.:** 2 hours
- **Acidity level:** Low; pressure canning required
- **Head Space:** 1 inch
- **Jar and Lid Preparation:** Sterilize jars and lids.
- **Procedure:** Sauté chopped leeks, then add diced potatoes and vegetable broth. Cook until potatoes are tender. Blend until smooth. Process in pressure canner for 75 minutes at 11 psi.
- **Ingr.:** 3 Cups potatoes, peeled and diced; 2 Cups leeks, chopped; 6 Cups vegetable broth.
- **Handling and Storage:** Store in a cool, dark place. Consume within a year.

Chicken and Vegetable Stew

- **P.T.:** 2 hours 30 minutes
- **Acidity level:** Low; pressure canning required
- **Head Space:** 1 inch
- **Jar and Lid Preparation:** Sterilize jars and lids.
- **Procedure:** Brown chicken pieces; add carrots, potatoes, onions, and chicken broth.

Cook until chicken is tender. Process in pressure canner for 90 minutes at 11 psi.

- **Ingr.:** 2 lb. chicken, cut into pieces; 2 Cups carrots, diced; 2 Cups potatoes, diced; 1 Cup onions, diced; 6 Cups chicken broth.
- **Handling and Storage:** Store in a cool, dark place. Use within a year.

Butternut Squash Soup

- **P.T.:** 2 hours
- **Acidity level:** Low; pressure canning required
- **Head Space:** 1 inch
- **Jar and Lid Preparation:** Sterilize jars and lids.

- **Procedure:** Roast butternut squash. Sauté onions and garlic, then add squash and vegetable broth. Blend until smooth. Process in pressure canner for 75 minutes at 11 psi.
- **Ingr.:** 4 Cups butternut squash, roasted and pureed; 1 Cup onions, chopped; 2 cloves garlic, minced; 6 Cups vegetable broth.

- **Handling and Storage:**
  Store in a cool, dark place.
  Consume within a
  year.Meat, Poultry, and
  Seafood Preservation
  Techniques

Chicken Soup Base

- **P.T.:** 2 hours 30 minutes
- **Acidity level:** Low
- **Head Space:** 1 inch
- **Jar and Lid Preparation:**
  Sterilize jars and lids.
- **Procedure:** Cook chicken
  pieces with carrots, celery,
  and onions in water. Strain
  broth, add back to
  shredded chicken. Fill jars
  and process at 11 psi for 75
  minutes.

- **Ingr.:** 2 lb. chicken pieces,
  1 Cup carrots, chopped; 1
  Cup celery, chopped; 1 Cup
  onions, chopped.
- **Handling and Storage:**
  Store in a cool, dark place;
  use within a year.

Spicy Sausage and Peppers

- **P.T.:** 3 hours
- **Acidity level:** Low
- **Head Space:** 1 inch
- **Jar and Lid Preparation:**
  Sterilize jars and lids.

- **Procedure:** Sauté sliced
  sausage with bell peppers
  and onions. Add tomato
  sauce and seasonings.
  Simmer, then fill jars and
  process at 11 psi for 75
  minutes.

- **Ingr.:** 2 lb. sausage, sliced; 2 Cups bell peppers, chopped; 1 Cup onions, chopped; 2 Cups tomato sauce.

- **Handling and Storage:** Store in a cool, dark place; use within a year.

Herb-Infused Pork Chops

- **P.T.:** 3 hours
- **Acidity level:** Low
- **Head Space:** 1 inch
- **Jar and Lid Preparation:** Sterilize jars and lids.
- **Procedure:** Brown pork chops with herbs. Deglaze with broth. Fill jars with pork and broth, process at 11 psi for 75 minutes.
- **Ingr.:** 4 pork chops; 1 Tblsp mixed herbs (thyme, rosemary, sage).
- **Handling and Storage:** Store in a cool, dark place; use within a year.

Turkey Chili

- **P.T.:** 3 hours
- **Acidity level:** Low
- **Head Space:** 1 inch
- **Jar and Lid Preparation:** Sterilize jars and lids.
- **Procedure:** Cook ground turkey with beans, tomatoes, onions, and chili spices. Simmer, then fill jars and process at 11 psi for 90 minutes.
- **Ingr.:** 2 lb. ground turkey; 1 Cup beans, prepared; 2 Cups tomatoes, chopped; Cup onions, chopped; 1 Tblsp chili powder.
- **Handling and Storage:** Store in a cool, dark place; use within a year.

Curried Lamb Stew

- **P.T.:** 3 hours 30 minutes
- **Acidity level:** Low
- **Head Space:** 1 inch
- **Jar and Lid Preparation:** Sterilize jars and lids.
- **Procedure:** Brown lamb pieces with curry spices. Add vegetables and coconut milk. Simmer, fill jars, and process at 11 psi for 90 minutes.
- **Ingr.:** 2 lb. lamb, cubed; 2 Cups mixed vegetables (carrots, potatoes, peas); 1 can coconut milk; 1 Tblsp curry powder.
- **Handling and Storage:** Store in a cool, dark place; use within a year.

Shrimp Creole

- **P.T.:** 2 hours 30 minutes
- **Acidity level:** Low
- **Head Space:** 1 inch
- **Jar and Lid Preparation:** Sterilize jars and lids.
- **Procedure:** Sauté shrimp, bell peppers, onions in Creole sauce. Cool, fill jars, and process at 11 psi for 60 minutes.
- **Ingr.:** 2 lb. shrimp, peeled; 1 Cup bell peppers, chopped; 1 Cup onions, chopped; 2 Cups Creole sauce.
- **Handling and Storage:** Store in a cool, dark place; use within 6 months.

Beef Bourguignon

- **P.T.:** 4 hours
- **Acidity level:** Low
- **Head Space:** 1 inch
- **Jar and Lid Preparation:** Sterilize jars and lids.
- **Procedure:** Sear beef chunks, cook with wine, broth, onions, mushrooms, and bacon. Simmer, fill jars, and process at 11 psi for 90 minutes.
- **Ingr.:** 2 lb. beef, cubed; 1 Cup onions, chopped; 1 Cup mushrooms, sliced; 1/2 Cups bacon, chopped; 2 Cups red wine; 2 Cups beef broth.
- **Handling and Storage:** Store in a cool, dark place; use within a year.

Venison Stew

- **P.T.:** 3 hours 30 minutes
- **Acidity level:** Low
- **Head Space:** 1 inch
- **Jar and Lid Preparation:** Sterilize jars and lids.
- **Procedure:** Brown venison with onions, carrots, potatoes. Add broth and seasonings. Fill jars and process at 11 psi for 90 minutes.
- **Ingr.:** 2 lb. venison, cubed 1 Cup carrots, chopped; 1 Cup potatoes, chopped; 1 Cup onions, chopped; 2 Cups beef broth.
- **Handling and Storage:** Store in a cool, dark place; use within a year.

Seafood Bisque

- **P.T.:** 2 hours
- **Acidity level:** Low
- **Head Space:** 1 inch
- **Jar and Lid Preparation:** Sterilize jars and lids.
- **Procedure:** Sauté a mix of seafood with onions, garlic in a creamy tomato broth. Cool, fill jars, and process at 11 psi for 60 minutes.
- **Ingr.:** 2 lb. mixed seafood (shrimp, crab, fish); 1 Cup onions, chopped; 2 cloves garlic, minced; 2 Cups tomato broth; 1 Cup cream.
- **Handling and Storage:** Store in a cool, dark place; use within 6 months.

Braised Rabbit with Vegetables

- **P.T.:** 3 hours
- **Acidity level:** Low
- **Head Space:** 1 inch
- **Jar and Lid Preparation:** Sterilize jars and lids.
- **Procedure:** Brown rabbit pieces, add root vegetables, broth, and herbs. Simmer until tender. Fill jars and process at 11 psi for 90 minutes.
- **Ingr.:** 1 rabbit, cut into pieces; 2 Cups root vegetables (carrots, parsnips); 2 Cups broth; 1 Tblsp mixed herbs (thyme, rosemary).
- **Handling and Storage:** Store in a cool, dark place; use within a year.

Classic Duck Confit

- **P.T.:** 4 hours
- **Acidity level:** Low
- **Head Space:** 1 inch
- **Jar and Lid Preparation:** Sterilize jars and lids.
- **Procedure:** Cure duck legs with salt, garlic, and herbs. Slow-cook in own fat. Cool, place in jars, and process at 11 psi for 100 minutes.
- **Ingr.:** 4 duck legs; 1 Tblsp salt; 2 cloves garlic, minced; 1 Tblsp mixed herbs (thyme, bay leaf).
- **Handling and Storage:** Store in a cool, dark place; use within a year.

Italian Sausage and Peppers

- **P.T.:** 2 hours 30 minutes
- **Acidity level:** Low
- **Head Space:** 1 inch
- **Jar and Lid Preparation:** Sterilize jars and lids.
- **Procedure:** Sauté Italian sausages with bell peppers, onions, and tomato sauce. Simmer, fill jars, and process at 11 psi for 75 minutes.
- **Ingr.:** 2 lb. Italian sausage sliced; 2 Cups bell peppers chopped; 1 Cup onions, chopped; 2 Cups tomato sauce.
- **Handling and Storage:** Store in a cool, dark place; use within a year.

Asian Pork Belly

- **P.T.:** 3 hours
- **Acidity level:** Low
- **Head Space:** 1 inch
- **Jar and Lid Preparation:** Sterilize jars and lids.
- **Procedure:** Braise pork belly with soy sauce, sugar, and Asian spices. Cook until tender. Fill jars and process at 11 psi for 90 minutes.

- **Ingr.:** 2 lb. pork belly; 1/4 Cups soy sauce; 1/4 Cups sugar; 1 Tblsp Asian spices (five-spice powder, garlic, ginger).
- **Handling and Storage:** Store in a cool, dark place; use within a year.

Mexican Chicken Tinga

- **P.T.:** 2 hours 30 minutes
- **Acidity level:** Low
- **Head Space:** 1 inch
- **Jar and Lid Preparation:** Sterilize jars and lids.
- **Procedure:** Cook shredded chicken with chipotle peppers, onions, and tomatoes. Simmer, fill jars, and process at 11 psi for 75 minutes.

- **Ingr.:** 2 lb. chicken, cooked and shredded; 1 Cup onions, chopped; 1 Cup tomatoes, chopped; 2 chipotle peppers in adobo sauce.
- **Handling and Storage:** Store in a cool, dark place; use within a year.

Moroccan Lamb Tagine

- **P.T.:** 3 hours 30 minutes
- **Acidity level:** Low
- **Head Space:** 1 inch
- **Jar and Lid Preparation:** Sterilize jars and lids.
- **Procedure:** Slow-cook lamb with apricots, onions, spices in a tagine. Cool, fill jars, and process at 11 psi for 90 minutes.
- **Ingr.:** 2 lb. lamb, cubed; 1 Cup dried apricots; 1 Cup onions, chopped; 1 Tblsp Moroccan spices (cumin, cinnamon, ginger).
- **Handling and Storage:** Store in a cool, dark place; use within a year.

Herbed Chicken Thighs

- **P.T.:** 2 hours
- **Acidity level:** Low; pressure canning required
- **Head Space:** 1 inch
- **Jar and Lid Preparation:** Sterilize jars and lids.
- **Procedure:** Season chicken thighs with a blend of herbs and garlic. Brown in a skillet. Pack into jars and cover with chicken broth. Process in pressure canner for 75 minutes at 11 psi.
- **Ingr.:** 4 chicken thighs; 1 Tblsp mixed herbs (thyme, rosemary, sage); 2 Cups chicken broth.
- **Handling and Storage:** Store in a cool, dark place. Consume within a year.

Savory Turkey Chili

- **P.T.:** 2 hours 30 minutes
- **Acidity level:** Low; pressure canning required
- **Head Space:** 1 inch
- **Jar and Lid Preparation:** Sterilize jars and lids.
- **Procedure:** Brown ground turkey with onions and garlic. Add tomatoes, beans, and chili spices. Simmer, then pack into jars. Process in pressure canner for 90 minutes at 11 psi.
- **Ingr.:** 2 lb. ground turkey; 1 Cup beans, prepared; 2 Cups tomatoes, chopped; 1 Tblsp chili spices.
- **Handling and Storage:** Store in a cool, dark place. Consume within a year.

Pork Carnitas

- **P.T.:** 3 hours
- **Acidity level:** Low; pressure canning required
- **Head Space:** 1 inch
- **Jar and Lid Preparation:** Sterilize jars and lids.
- **Procedure:** Season pork shoulder with a blend of Mexican spices. Slow cook until tender. Shred the pork and pack into jars, adding some of the cooking liquid. Process in pressure canner for 75 minutes at 11 psi.
- **Ingr.:** 2 lb. pork shoulder; 1 Tblsp Mexican spices (cumin, chili powder, garlic).

- **Handling and Storage:**

  Store in a cool, dark place.

  Consume within a year.

Asian-Style Beef Ribs

- **P.T.:** 3 hours
- **Acidity level:** Low; pressure canning required
- **Head Space:** 1 inch
- **Jar and Lid Preparation:** Sterilize jars and lids.
- **Procedure:** Marinate beef ribs in a mixture of soy sauce, rice wine, garlic, ginger, and sesame oil for 2 hours. Brown the ribs in a skillet. Place ribs in jars, adding the marinade and beef broth. Process in pressure canner for 90 minutes at 11 psi.
- **Ingr.:** 2 lb. beef ribs; 1/4 Cups soy sauce; 1/4 Cups rice wine; 2 cloves garlic, minced; 1 Tblsp ginger, grated; 1 tsp sesame oil; 2 Cups beef broth.
- **Handling and Storage:** Store in a cool, dark place. Consume within a year.

Combining Foods: Creating Balanced Meals in a Jar

Moroccan Chickpea and Vegetable Stew

- **P.T.:** 2 hours 45 minutes
- **Acidity level:** Low; pressure canning required
- **Head Space:** 1 inch
- **Jar and Lid Preparation:** Sterilize jars and lids.
- **Procedure:** Sauté onions, garlic, and spices (cumin, coriander, cinnamon). Add chickpeas, diced tomatoes, carrots, and vegetable broth. Simmer for 1 hour. Process in pressure canner for 85 minutes at 11 psi.
- **Ingr.:** 2 Cups chickpeas, soaked and cooked; 1 Cup onions, chopped; 2 cloves garlic, minced; 1 tsp cumin; 1 tsp coriander; 1/2 tsp cinnamon; 2 Cups diced tomatoes; 1 Cup carrots, chopped; 4 Cups vegetable broth.
- **Handling and Storage:** Store in a cool, dark place. Use within a year.

Beef and Barley Soup

- **P.T.:** 3 hours
- **Acidity level:** Low; pressure canning required
- **Head Space:** 1 inch
- **Jar and Lid Preparation:** Sterilize jars and lids.
- **Procedure:** Brown beef chunks; add barley, diced onions, carrots, celery, and beef broth. Cook until barley is tender. Process in pressure canner for 90 minutes at 11 psi.
- **Ingr.:** 2 lb. beef, cubed; 1 Cup barley, rinsed; 1 Cup onions, chopped; 1 Cup carrots, chopped; 1 Cup celery, chopped; 6 Cups beef broth.

- **Handling and Storage:**
  Store in a cool, dark place.
  Consume within a year.

Chicken Curry with Vegetables

- **P.T.:** 2 hours 30 minutes
- **Acidity level:** Low;
  pressure canning required
- **Head Space:** 1 inch
- **Jar and Lid Preparation:**
  Sterilize jars and lids.
- **Procedure:** Sauté diced
  chicken, onions, and curry
  spices. Add coconut milk,
  diced potatoes, carrots, and
  peas.
  Simmer for 30 minutes.
  Process in pressure canner
  for 75 minutes at 11 psi.
- **Ingr.:** 2 lb. chicken, diced;
  1 Cup onions, chopped; 1
  Tblsp curry powder; 1 can
  coconut milk; 1 Cup
  potatoes, diced; 1 Cup
  carrots, chopped; 1/2 Cups
  peas.
- **Handling and Storage:**
  Store in a cool, dark place.
  Use within a year.

Vegetarian Quinoa Chili

- **P.T.:** 2 hours
- **Acidity level:** Low;
  pressure canning required
- **Head Space:** 1 inch
- **Jar and Lid Preparation:**
  Sterilize jars and lids.
- **Procedure:** Cook quinoa,
  black beans, corn, bell
  peppers, onions, tomatoes,
  and chili spices in vegetable
  broth. Simmer for 45
  minutes. Process in
  pressure canner for 75
  minutes at 11 psi.

- **Ingr.:** 1 Cup quinoa, rinsed; 1 Cup black beans, soaked and cooked; 1 Cup corn; 1 Cup bell peppers, chopped; 1 Cup onions, chopped; 2 Cups tomatoes, chopped; 2 Tblsp chili powder; 4 Cups vegetable broth.

- **Handling and Storage:** Store in a cool, dark place. Use within a year.

Tuscan White Bean and Kale Soup

- **P.T.:** 2 hours 30 minutes
- **Acidity level:** Low; pressure canning required
- **Head Space:** 1 inch
- **Jar and Lid Preparation:** Sterilize jars and lids.
- **Procedure:** Sauté garlic and onions. Add soaked white beans, chopped kale, carrots, celery, and chicken broth. Cook until beans are tender. Process in pressure canner for 90 minutes at 11 psi.

- **Ingr.:** 2 Cups white beans, soaked; 1 Cup kale, chopped; 1 Cup carrots, chopped; 1 Cup celery, chopped; 2 cloves garlic, minced; 1 Cup onions, chopped; 6 Cups chicken broth.

- **Handling and Storage:** Store in a cool, dark place. Consume within a year.

Seafood Paella

- **P.T.:** 2 hours 30 minutes
- **Acidity level:** Low; pressure canning required
- **Head Space:** 1 inch
- **Jar and Lid Preparation:** Sterilize jars and lids.
- **Procedure:** Cook rice with saffron, garlic, onions, bell peppers, tomatoes, shrimp, mussels, and chicken broth. Simmer for 40 minutes. Process in pressure canner for 60 minutes at 11 psi.
- **Ingr.:** 1 Cup rice; 1 pinch saffron; 2 cloves garlic, minced; 1 Cup onions chopped; 1 Cup bell peppers, chopped; 1 Cup tomatoes, chopped; 1 lb. shrimp; 1/2 lb. mussels; 4 Cups chicken broth.
- **Handling and Storage:** Store in a cool, dark place. Use within six months.

Pork and Sweet Potato Stew

- **P.T.:** 3 hours
- **Acidity level:** Low; pressure canning required
- **Head Space:** 1 inch
- **Jar and Lid Preparation:** Sterilize jars and lids.
- **Procedure:** Brown pork cubes; add cubed sweet potatoes, onions, apple cider, and spices. Cook until pork is tender. Process in pressure canner for 90 minutes at 11 psi.
- **Ingr.:** 2 lb. pork, cubed; 2 Cups sweet potatoes, cubed; 1 Cup onions, chopped; 1 Cup apple cider; 1 tsp cinnamon; 1/2 tsp nutmeg.
- **Handling and Storage:** Store in a cool, dark place. Consume within a year.

Spicy Lentil and Sausage Soup

- **P.T.:** 2 hours 45 minutes
- **Acidity level:** Low; pressure canning required
- **Head Space:** 1 inch
- **Jar and Lid Preparation:** Sterilize jars and lids.
- **Procedure:** Cook lentils, sliced sausage, diced tomatoes, carrots, onions, and spicy broth. Simmer for 1 hour. Process in pressure canner for 75 minutes at 11 psi.
- **Ingr.:** 1 Cup lentils, rinsed; 1 lb. sausage, sliced; 2 Cups diced tomatoes; 1 Cup carrots, chopped; 1 Cup onions, chopped; 2 tsp chili flakes; 4 Cups spicy broth.
- **Handling and Storage:** Store in a cool, dark place. Use within a year.

Ratatouille

- **P.T.:** 2 hours
- **Acidity level:** Low; pressure canning required
- **Head Space:** 1 inch
- **Jar and Lid Preparation:** Sterilize jars and lids.
- **Procedure:** Layer sliced eggplant, zucchini, bell peppers, onions, and tomatoes with herbs and olive oil. Simmer for 30 minutes. Process in pressure canner for 60 minutes at 11 psi.
- **Ingr.:** 1 Cup eggplant, sliced; 1 Cup zucchini, sliced; 1 Cup bell peppers, sliced; 1 Cup onions, sliced; 2 Cups tomatoes, sliced; 2 Tblsp olive oil; 1 Tblsp mixed herbs (thyme, rosemary).
- **Handling and Storage:** Store in a cool, dark place. Use within a year.

Beef Goulash

- **P.T.:** 3 hours
- **Acidity level:** Low; pressure canning required

- **Head Space:** 1 inch
- **Jar and Lid Preparation:** Sterilize jars and lids.
- **Procedure:** Brown beef chunks with onions, paprika, and garlic. Add diced tomatoes and beef broth. Simmer for 1 hour. Process in pressure canner for 90 minutes at 11 psi.
- **Ingr.:** 2 lb. beef, cubed; 1 Cup onions, chopped; 2 Tblsp paprika; 2 cloves garlic, minced; 2 Cups diced tomatoes; 4 Cups beef broth.
- **Handling and Storage:** Store in a cool, dark place. Consume within a year.

Chicken Tagine with Apricots

- **P.T.:** 3 hours
- **Acidity level:** Low; pressure canning required
- **Head Space:** 1 inch
- **Jar and Lid Preparation:** Sterilize jars and lids.
- **Procedure:** Brown chicken pieces with onions, ginger, and spices. Add dried apricots and chicken broth. Simmer for 1 hour. Process in pressure canner for 75 minutes at 11 psi.
- **Ingr.:** 2 lb. chicken, cut into pieces; 1 Cup onions, sliced; 1 Tblsp ginger, minced; 1 tsp cinnamon; 1/2 Cups dried apricots; 4 Cups chicken broth.
- **Handling and Storage:** Store in a cool, dark place. Use within a year.

Vegetarian Borscht

- **P.T.:** 2 hours 30 minutes
- **Acidity level:** Low; pressure canning required
- **Head Space:** 1 inch
- **Jar and Lid Preparation:** Sterilize jars and lids.
- **Procedure:** Cook beets, carrots, potatoes, cabbage, onions, and vegetable broth. Add a splash of vinegar. Simmer for 1 hour. Process in pressure canner for 75 minutes at 11 psi.
- **Ingr.:** 2 Cups beets, chopped; 1 Cup carrots, chopped; 1 Cup potatoes, chopped; 1 Cup cabbage, chopped; 1 Cup onions, chopped; 4 Cups vegetable broth; 2 Tblsp vinegar.
- **Handling and Storage:** Store in a cool, dark place. Use within a year.

Coq au Vin

- **P.T.:** 3 hours
- **Acidity level:** Low; pressure canning required
- **Head Space:** 1 inch
- **Jar and Lid Preparation:** Sterilize jars and lids.
- **Procedure:** Brown chicken pieces, add mushrooms, onions, garlic, and red wine. Simmer for 1 hour. Process in pressure canner for 75 minutes at 11 psi.
- **Ingr.:** 2 lb. chicken, cut into pieces; 1 Cup mushrooms, sliced; 1 Cup onions, chopped; 2 cloves garlic, minced; 2 Cups red wine; 4 Cups chicken broth.
- **Handling and Storage:** Store in a cool, dark place. Use within a year.

Spicy Bean and Rice Burrito Filling

- **P.T.:** 2 hours 45 minutes
- **Acidity level:** Low; pressure canning required
- **Head Space:** 1 inch
- **Jar and Lid Preparation:** Sterilize jars and lids.

- **Procedure:** Cook rice, black beans, corn, bell peppers, onions, and Mexican spices. Add tomat sauce. Simmer for 45 minutes. Process in pressure canner for 70 minutes at 11 psi.
- **Ingr.:** 1 Cup rice, cooked; 1 Cup black beans, cooked 1 Cup corn; 1 Cup bell peppers, chopped; 1 Cup onions, chopped; 2 Tblsp Mexican spices; 2 Cups tomato sauce.
- **Handling and Storage:** Store in a cool, dark place. Use within a year.

Thai Green Curry with Chicken

- **P.T.:** 2 hours 30 minutes
- **Acidity level:** Low; pressure canning required
- **Head Space:** 1 inch
- **Jar and Lid Preparation:** Sterilize jars and lids.

- **Procedure:** Sauté chicken with Thai green curry paste coconut milk, bamboo shoots, and vegetables. Simmer for 30 minutes. Process in pressure canner for 60 minutes at 11 psi.

- **Ingr.:** 2 lb. chicken, cut into pieces; 2 Tblsp Thai green curry paste; 1 can coconut milk; 1 Cup bamboo shoots; 2 Cups mixed vegetables (bell peppers, peas).

- **Handling and Storage:** Store in a cool, dark place. Use within six months.

Seafood Gumbo

- **P.T.:** 2 hours 45 minutes
- **Acidity level:** Low; pressure canning required
- **Head Space:** 1 inch
- **Jar and Lid Preparation:** Sterilize jars and lids.
- **Procedure:** Make a roux with flour and oil. Add onions, celery, bell peppers, and okra. Stir in seafood, chicken broth, and Cajun spices. Simmer for 1 hour. Process in pressure canner for 75 minutes at 11 psi.

- **Ingr.:** 1/4 Cups flour; 1/4 Cups oil; 1 Cup onions, chopped; 1 Cup celery, chopped; 1 Cup bell peppers, chopped; 1 Cup okra, chopped; 1 lb. mixed seafood (shrimp, crab); 4 Cups chicken broth; 2 Tblsp Cajun spices.

- **Handling and Storage:** Store in a cool, dark place. Use within six months.

Jambalaya

- **P.T.:** 2 hours 30 minutes
- **Acidity level:** Low; pressure canning required
- **Head Space:** 1 inch

- **Jar and Lid Preparation:** Sterilize jars and lids.

- **Procedure:** Cook chicken, sausage, shrimp, rice, tomatoes, onions, bell peppers, and Cajun seasoning. Simmer for 40 minutes. Process in pressure canner for 70 minutes at 11 psi.
- **Ingr.:** 1 lb. chicken, chopped; 1 lb. sausage, chopped; 1/2 lb. shrimp, prepared; 1 Cup rice; 2 Cups tomatoes, chopped; 1 Cup onions, chopped; 1 Cup bell peppers, chopped; 2 Tblsp Cajun seasoning.
- **Handling and Storage:** Store in a cool, dark place. Use within a year.

Pork and Beans

- **P.T.:** 3 hours
- **Acidity level:** Low; pressure canning required
- **Head Space:** 1 inch
- **Jar and Lid Preparation:** Sterilize jars and lids.
- **Procedure:** Brown pork chunks; add soaked navy beans, onions, tomato sauce, molasses, and spices. Simmer for 1 hour 30 minutes. Process in pressure canner for 90 minutes at 11 psi.
- **Ingr.:** 2 lb. pork, cubed; 2 Cups navy beans, soaked; Cup onions, chopped; 2 Cups tomato sauce; 1/4 Cups molasses; 1 Tblsp mixed spices.
- **Handling and Storage:** Store in a cool, dark place. Use within a year.

Mediterranean Lamb Stew

- **P.T.:** 3 hours
- **Acidity level:** Low; pressure canning required
- **Head Space:** 1 inch
- **Jar and Lid Preparation:** Sterilize jars and lids.
- **Procedure:** Brown lamb cubes and sauté with onions, garlic, and Mediterranean herbs (rosemary, thyme). Add diced tomatoes, olives, and a splash of red wine. Simmer for 1 hour 30 minutes. Process in pressure canner for 90 minutes at 11 psi.
- **Ingr.:** 2 lb. lamb, cubed; 1 Cup onions, chopped; 2 cloves garlic, minced; 1 Tblsp mixed Mediterranean herbs; 2 Cups diced tomatoes; 1/2 Cups olives; 1/4 Cups red wine.
- **Handling and Storage:** Store in a cool, dark place. Consume within a year.
-

Southwest Chicken and Corn Chowder

- **P.T.:** 2 hours 30 minutes
- **Acidity level:** Low; pressure canning required
- **Head Space:** 1 inch
- **Jar and Lid Preparation:** Sterilize jars and lids.
- **Procedure:** Sauté diced chicken, onions, bell peppers, and Southwest spices (cumin, paprika). Add corn kernels, diced potatoes, and chicken broth. Cook until vegetables are tender. Process in pressure canner for 75 minutes at 11 psi.

- **Ingr.:** 2 lb. chicken, diced; 1 Cup onions, chopped; 1 Cup bell peppers, chopped; 2 tsp cumin; 2 tsp paprika; 2 Cups corn kernels; 1 Cup potatoes, diced; 4 Cups chicken broth.
- **Handling and Storage:** Store in a cool, dark place. Use within a year.

Book IV: Alternative Preservation Methods

Fermenting Foods: Health Benefits and Basic Recipes

At the heart of fermentation lies the principle of microbial magic. Beneficial bacteria, yeasts, and molds engage in a transformative process, converting sugars and starches into acids, gases, or alcohol. This natural phenomenon not only imparts unique flavors and textures but also enhances the nutritional profile of the food. Fermented foods are often rich in probiotics, those friendly microbes that play a crucial role in gut health, digestion, and even bolstering the immune system.

Beyond its health benefits, the world of fermentation is a realm of unparalleled culinary diversity. From the tangy complexity of a well-aged cheese to the refreshing effervescence of kombucha, from the piquant zing of kimchi to the mellow savoriness of miso – each fermented food is a testament to the rich cultural heritages that have nurtured these practices through generations.

To embark on the journey of fermentation is to engage in an age-old practice that predates recorded history. Our ancestors, guided by observation and intuition, harnessed fermentation to preserve perishable foods in times of abundance. This wisdom, passed down through the ages, has culminated in a myriad of fermentation techniques across different cultures – each method a reflection of the environment, climate, and local produce that gave birth to it.

Classic Sauerkraut

- **P.T.:** 20 minutes (fermentation time: 2-4 weeks)
- **Acidity level:** N/A for fermentation
- **Procedure:** Shred cabbage and mix with salt. Massage until brine forms. Pack tightly in a jar, ensuring cabbage is submerged in brine. Cover and allow to ferment at room temperature.
- **Ingr.:** 1 medium cabbage, shredded; 1 Tblsp salt.
- **Handling and Storage:** Store at room temperature during fermentation, then refrigerate.

Kimchi

- **P.T.:** 45 minutes (fermentation time: 1-2 weeks)
- **Procedure:** Mix chopped Napa cabbage and Korean radish with a paste of garlic, ginger, fish sauce, and Korean red pepper flakes. Ferment at room temperature, then store in the refrigerator.
- **Ingr.:** 1 Napa cabbage, chopped; 1 Korean radish, chopped; 4 cloves garlic, minced; 1 inch ginger, minced; 2 Tblsp fish sauce; 4 Tblsp Korean red pepper flakes.
- **Handling and Storage:** Room temperature for initial fermentation, then refrigerate.

Kombucha

- **P.T.:** 30 minutes (fermentation time: 7-14 days)
- **Procedure:** Brew black tea and dissolve sugar in it. Cool to room temperature. Add SCOBY and starter tea. Cover with a cloth and ferment. After fermenting, can flavor with fruit or herbs.
- **Ingr.:** 4 black tea bags; 1 Cup sugar; 1 SCOBY; 2 Cups starter tea.
- **Handling and Storage:** Ferment at room temperature, then refrigerate after bottling.

Fermented Carrot Sticks

- **P.T.:** 20 minutes (fermentation time: 3-5 days)
- **Procedure:** Slice carrots into sticks. Mix with water, salt, and optional spices (garlic, dill). Ensure carrots are submerged. Cover and let ferment at room temperature.
- **Ingr.:** 5 large carrots, sliced into sticks; 2 tsp salt 4 Cups water; Optional: garlic cloves, dill.
- **Handling and Storage:** Ferment at room temperature, then refrigerate.

Sourdough Starter

- **P.T.:** 10 minutes daily (fermentation time: 5-7 days)

- **Procedure:** Mix equal parts flour and water. Cover and let sit at room temperature. Feed daily with equal parts flour and water.

- **Ingr.:** 1 Cup flour; 1 Cup water.

- **Handling and Storage:** Keep at room temperature, feed daily.

Ginger Bug (for Homemade Sodas)

- **P.T.:** 15 minutes daily (fermentation time: 5 days)

- **Procedure:** Mix chopped ginger, sugar, and water in a jar. Stir daily. After bubbles form, it can be used to ferment homemade sodas.

- **Ingr.:** 2 Tblsp ginger, chopped; 2 Tblsp sugar; 2 Cups water.

- **Handling and Storage:** Ferment at room temperature, then use in soda recipes.

Beet Kvass

- **P.T.:** 15 minutes (fermentation time: 5-7 days)
- **Procedure:** Chop beets and place in a jar. Add salt, water, and optional starter culture. Cover and let ferment, then transfer to the refrigerator.
- **Ingr.:** 3 medium beets, chopped; 1 Tblsp salt; 4 Cups water; Optional: starter culture.
- **Handling and Storage:** Ferment at room temperature, then refrigerate.

Lacto-Fermented Lemons

- **P.T.:** 20 minutes (fermentation time: 3-4 weeks)
- **Procedure:** Quarter lemons, leaving them attached at the base. Pack with salt and place in a jar. Press to release juice. Ferment, then refrigerate.
- **Ingr.:** 4 lemons; 1/4 Cups salt.
- **Handling and Storage:** Ferment at room temperature, then refrigerate.

Fermented Hot Sauce

- **P.T.:** 30 minutes (fermentation time: 1-2 weeks)
- **Procedure:** Blend hot peppers with garlic, salt, and water to form a paste. Ferment at room temperature, then blend again and strain. Store in refrigerator.
- **Ingr.:** 1 lb. hot peppers; 4 cloves garlic; 1 Tblsp salt; 2 Cups water.
- **Handling and Storage:** Ferment at room temperature, then refrigerate.

Miso Fermented Vegetables

- **P.T.:** 30 minutes (fermentation time: 1-2 weeks)
- **Procedure:** Mix chopped vegetables (carrots, cucumbers, radishes) with miso paste. Pack into a jar, ensuring vegetables are coated. Ferment, then refrigerate.
- **Ingr.:** 2 Cups mixed vegetables (carrots, cucumbers, radishes); 1/2 Cups miso paste.
- **Handling and Storage:** Ferment at room temperature, then refrigerate.

Fermented Garlic Honey

- **P.T.:** 20 minutes (fermentation time: 1 month)
- **Procedure:** Fill a jar with peeled garlic cloves and completely cover with raw honey. Stir occasionally. Ferment at room temperature until garlic is infused into the honey.
- **Ingr.:** 1 Cup garlic cloves, peeled; 1 Cup raw honey.
- **Handling and Storage:** Store at room temperature during fermentation, then refrigerate.

Pineapple Tepache

- **P.T.:** 30 minutes (fermentation time: 3-5 days)
- **Procedure:** Combine pineapple rinds, brown sugar, and water in a jar. Cover loosely and ferment at room temperature. Strain and refrigerate.
- **Ingr.:** Peel of 1 pineapple; 1 Cup brown sugar; 8 Cups water.
- **Handling and Storage:** Ferment at room temperature, then refrigerate.

Fermented Cranberry Sauce

- **P.T.:** 25 minutes (fermentation time: 3-4 days)
- **Procedure:** Mash cranberries with sugar and orange zest. Add a cinnamon stick and water. Cover and let ferment. Once fermented, refrigerate.
- **Ingr.:** 2 Cups cranberries; 1/2 Cups sugar; Zest of 1 orange; 1 cinnamon stick; 2 Cups water.
- **Handling and Storage:** Ferment at room temperature, then refrigerate.

Traditional Russian Kvass

- **P.T.:** 1 hour (fermentation time: 5-7 days)
- **Procedure:** Soak rye bread in water; add sugar and yeast. Ferment for several days, stirring daily. Strain and refrigerate.
- **Ingr.:** 4 slices rye bread, toasted; 1/4 Cups sugar; 1 tsp yeast; 8 Cups water.
- **Handling and Storage:** Ferment at room temperature, then refrigerate.

Fermented Mango Chutney

- **P.T.:** 40 minutes (fermentation time: 1 week)
- **Procedure:** Mix chopped mango, onion, chili, spices, and salt. Pack into a jar, ensuring it's submerged in its juice. Ferment, then refrigerate.

- **Ingr.:** 2 mangoes, chopped; 1 onion, chopped 1 chili, chopped; 1 tsp each of cumin and coriander; 1 Tblsp salt.
- **Handling and Storage:** Ferment at room temperature, then refrigerate.

Water Kefir

- **P.T.:** 15 minutes (fermentation time: 24-48 hours)
- **Procedure:** Dissolve sugar in water. Add water kefir grains and optional dried fruits. Ferment for 24-48 hours, then strain and refrigerate.

- **Ingr.:** 1/4 Cups sugar; 4 Cups water; 1/4 Cups water kefir grains; Optional: dried fruits.
- **Handling and Storage:** Ferment at room temperature, then refrigerate.

Japanese Natto

- **P.T.:** 1 hour (fermentation time: 24 hours)
- **Procedure:** Soak soybeans overnight, steam until tender. Mix with natto spores. Ferment in a warm place, then refrigerate.
- **Ingr.:** 2 Cups soybeans; 1/4 tsp natto spores.
- **Handling and Storage:** Ferment in a warm place, then refrigerate.

Fermented Sriracha Sauce

- **P.T.:** 30 minutes (fermentation time: 5-7 days)
- **Procedure:** Blend red chilies, garlic, sugar, and salt. Ferment the mixture, stirring daily. Blend again until smooth, then strain and refrigerate.
- **Ingr.:** 1 lb. red chilies; 6 cloves garlic; 2 Tblsp sugar; 2 tsp salt.
- **Handling and Storage:** Ferment at room temperature, then refrigerate.

Cultured Mustard

- **P.T.:** 20 minutes (fermentation time: 2-3 days)
- **Procedure:** Mix mustard seeds, mustard powder, water, and a starter culture. Ferment at room temperature, then blend and refrigerate.
- **Ingr.:** 1/4 Cups mustard seeds; 1/4 Cups mustard powder; 1/2 Cups water; Starter culture (optional).
- **Handling and Storage:** Ferment at room temperature, then refrigerate.

Fermented Beet Kvass

- **P.T.:** 30 minutes (fermentation time: 5-7 days)
- **Procedure:** Chop beets and place in a jar with salt and filtered water. Add optional flavorings like ginger or lemon. Ferment, then refrigerate.
- **Ingr.:** 3 medium beets, chopped; 1 Tblsp salt; 4 Cups filtered water; Optional: ginger slice, lemon wedge.
- **Handling and Storage:** Ferment at room temperature, then refrigerate.

Dehydrating Fruits, Vegetables, and Meats: Techniques and Tips

The beauty of dehydration lies in its elemental simplicity and the transformative effect it has on food. When water is removed, flavors intensify, textures transform, and the shelf life of foods is extended remarkably. This process not only preserves the bounty of gardens and harvests but also provides a way to enjoy the flavors of seasons long past.

Fruits, with their natural sweetness and vibrant flavors, become jewels of flavor when dehydrated. Apples turn into crisp, sweet chips, berries become bursts of concentrated delight, and tropical fruits like pineapples and mangoes transform into chewy, candy-like treats. Vegetables, too, undergo a remarkable metamorphosis – mushrooms take on a meaty texture, peppers become intensely flavored morsels, and tomatoes emerge as rich, savory sun-dried wonders.

Dehydrating meats opens up a realm of possibilities. Jerky, a time-honored favorite, is made by marinating thin slices of meat and drying them until they are leathery yet pliable. This method, which originated as a necessity, has now become a beloved snack, appreciated for its rich flavor and satisfying texture.

The process of dehydration can be as simple as air-drying in the sun, a method used for centuries in warmer climes, or as modern as using an electric dehydrator, which offers more control over temperature and air flow. The key to successful dehydration lies in the balance of temperature and time. Too high a temperature can cook food instead of drying it, while too low can allow bacteria to grow.

Crispy Apple Chips

- **P.T.:** 15 minutes prep, 6-8 hours dehydration
- **Procedure:** Thinly slice apples and arrange on dehydrator trays. Dehydrate at 135°F until crisp, about 6-8 hours.
- **Ingr.:** 4 large apples.
- **Handling and Storage:** Store in an airtight container in a cool, dark place.

Sweet Potato Dog Treats

- **P.T.:** 20 minutes prep, 6-8 hours dehydration
- **Procedure:** Slice sweet potatoes thinly and arrange on dehydrator trays. Dehydrate at 145°F until chewy, about 6-8 hours.
- **Ingr.:** 2 large sweet potatoes.
- **Handling and Storage:** Keep in an airtight container.

Spicy Beef Jerky

- **P.T.:** 1 hour prep, 4-6 hours dehydration
- **Procedure:** Marinate thin strips of beef in a mixture of soy sauce, Worcestershire sauce, and spices. Dehydrate at 160°F until dry, about 4-6 hours.
- **Ingr.:** 2 lb. beef (top round or similar),; 1/2 Cups soy sauce,; 1/4 Cups Worcestershire sauce,; 1 Tblsp chili powder,; 1 tsp garlic powder,; 1 tsp onion powder.
- **Handling and Storage:** Store jerky in a cool, dry place.

Zesty Lemon Zest

- **P.T.:** 10 minutes prep, 6-8 hours dehydration
- **Procedure:** Grate the zest of lemons and spread on a dehydrator sheet. Dehydrate at 95°F until completely dry.
- **Ingr.:** 5 large lemons.
- **Handling and Storage:** Store in an airtight container in a cool, dark place.

Herb-Infused Tomato Slices

- **P.T.:** 15 minutes prep, 8-10 hours dehydration
- **Procedure:** Slice tomatoes and sprinkle with basil, oregano, and salt. Dehydrate at 135°F until fully dried.
- **Ingr.:** 4 large tomatoes,; tsp dried basil,; 1 tsp dried oregano,; 1/2 tsp salt.
- **Handling and Storage:** Store in an airtight container.

Homemade Banana Chips

- **P.T.:** 20 minutes prep, 6-8 hours dehydration
- **Procedure:** Slice bananas and dip in lemon juice. Arrange on dehydrator trays. Dehydrate at 135°F until crisp.
- **Ingr.:** 5 ripe bananas,; 1/4 Cups lemon juice.
- **Handling and Storage:** Keep in an airtight container.

Spicy Kale Chips

- **P.T.:** 15 minutes prep, 4-6 hours dehydration
- **Procedure:** Tear kale into bite-sized pieces and toss with olive oil, chili powder, and salt. Dehydrate at 125°F until crispy.
- **Ingr.:** 1 bunch kale,; 2 Tblsp olive oil,; 1 tsp chili powder,; 1/2 tsp salt.
- **Handling and Storage:** Store in an airtight container.

Savory Mushroom Powder

- **P.T.:** 30 minutes prep, 8-10 hours dehydration
- **Procedure:** Thinly slice mushrooms and dehydrate at 125°F until completely dry. Grind into a fine powder.
- **Ingr.:** 1 lb. mushrooms.
- **Handling and Storage:** Store powder in a dark, cool place.

Dried Pineapple Rings

- **P.T.:** 20 minutes prep, 8-10 hours dehydration
- **Procedure:** Slice pineapple into rings and remove the core. Dehydrate at 135°F until fully dried.
- **Ingr.:** 1 large pineapple.
- **Handling and Storage:** Keep in an airtight container.

Venison Jerky

- **P.T.:** 1 hour prep, 5-7 hours dehydration
- **Procedure:** Marinate thin strips of venison in a mixture of soy sauce, black pepper, and garlic powder. Dehydrate at 160°F until dry.
- **Ingr.:** 2 lb. venison,; 1/2 Cups soy sauce,; 1 tsp black pepper,; 1 tsp garlic powder.
- **Handling and Storage:** Store in a cool, dry place.

Ginger-Infused Pear Slices

- **P.T.:** 20 minutes prep, 6-8 hours dehydration
- **Procedure:** Slice pears thinly and sprinkle with ground ginger. Arrange on dehydrator trays and dehydrate at 135°F until crisp.
- **Ingr.:** 4 large pears,; 1 tsp ground ginger.
- **Handling and Storage:** Store in an airtight container in a cool, dark place.

Dried Chili Flakes

- **P.T.:** 15 minutes prep, 6-8 hours dehydration
- **Procedure:** Slice chili peppers and remove seeds. Dehydrate at 125°F until completely dry. Crush into flakes.
- **Ingr.:** 1/2 lb. chili peppers.
- **Handling and Storage:** Store in an airtight, dry container.

Garlic and Herb Seasoned Tomatoes

- **P.T.:** 30 minutes prep, 8-10 hours dehydration
- **Procedure:** Slice tomatoes and sprinkle with a mix of crushed garlic, basil, and oregano. Dehydrate at 135°F.
- **Ingr.:** 4 large tomatoes,; 2 cloves garlic, minced,; 1 tsp dried basil,; 1 tsp dried oregano.
- **Handling and Storage:** Keep in an airtight container.

Citrus Peel Powder

- **P.T.:** 10 minutes prep, 6-8 hours dehydration
- **Procedure:** Peel oranges, lemons, and limes. Dehydrate peels at 95°F until dry. Grind into a fine powder.
- **Ingr.:** 2 oranges,; 2 lemons,; 2 limes.
- **Handling and Storage:** Store in a cool, dark place in an airtight container.

Dried Mango Slices

- **P.T.:** 20 minutes prep, 10-12 hours dehydration
- **Procedure:** Slice mangoes thinly. Dehydrate at 135°F until leathery.

- **Ingr.:** 3 large mangoes.
- **Handling and Storage:** Store in an airtight container.

Crunchy Green Bean Snacks

- **P.T.:** 15 minutes prep, 8-10 hours dehydration
- **Procedure:** Trim green beans and blanch briefly. Dehydrate at 125°F until crisp.

- **Ingr.:** 1 lb. green beans.
- **Handling and Storage:** Keep in an airtight container.

Dried Strawberry Slices

- **P.T.:** 20 minutes prep, 6-8 hours dehydration
- **Procedure:** Slice strawberries and arrange on dehydrator trays. Dehydrate at 135°F until crisp.

- **Ingr.:** 2 lb. strawberries.
- **Handling and Storage:** Store in an airtight container.

Turkey Jerky Strips

- **P.T.:** 1 hour prep, 5-7 hours dehydration
- **Procedure:** Slice turkey breast thinly and marinate in a mixture of soy sauce, liquid smoke, and spices. Dehydrate at 160°F until dry.
- **Ingr.:** 2 lb. turkey breast,; 1/2 Cups soy sauce,; 1 Tblsp liquid smoke,; 1 tsp paprika,; 1 tsp black pepper.
- **Handling and Storage:** Store in a cool, dry place.

Dried Blueberries

- **P.T.:** 20 minutes prep, 10-12 hours dehydration
- **Procedure:** Blanch blueberries to crack skins. Dehydrate at 135°F until they reach a raisin-like consistency.
- **Ingr.:** 2 lb. blueberries.
- **Handling and Storage:** Store in an airtight container.

Spiced Carrot Chips

- **P.T.:** 20 minutes prep, 6-8 hours dehydration
- **Procedure:** Slice carrots thinly. Toss with olive oil, cinnamon, and nutmeg. Dehydrate at 125°F until crisp.

- **Ingr.:** 1 lb. carrots,; 2 Tblsp olive oil,; 1 tsp cinnamon,; 1/2 tsp nutmeg.
- **Handling and Storage:** Keep in an airtight container.

Pickling: Beyond Cucumbers - Exploring Variety

Pickling is the ancient craft of preserving food in a brine or vinegar solution transforming ingredients into tangy delights. Perfect for cucumbers, onions, beets and more, this method uses acidity to prevent harmful microorganisms from thriving enhancing the natural flavors and textures of the produce. It's a dance of chemistry and culinary skill that preserves and elevates the food's character.

The process starts with selecting the freshest, highest-quality produce. Crisp cucumbers, vibrant peppers, and firm carrots ensure the best pickles. Preparation is meticulous: vegetables are cleaned, sometimes peeled, and cut uniformly to ensure even pickling. Spices and herbs like garlic, dill, mustard seeds, and peppercorns are carefully measured to create a balanced brine.

Packing the jars is an exercise in precision. Vegetables are layered and arranged for optimal contact with the pickling solution. The brine, a heated mixture of vinegar salt, and sometimes sugar and spices, is poured over the vegetables, filling the jar while leaving necessary headspace for expansion and sealing. The jars are then processed, often in a boiling water bath, to create a vacuum seal and inhibit microbial growth.

As the jars cool, the vegetables absorb the brine's flavors, becoming pickles. This resting period is essential for developing full flavor and texture. Stored in a cool, dark place these jars are culinary treasures, ready to add a zesty punch to meals. Each jar of pickles is a celebration of the seasons, a nod to tradition, and a showcase of self-sufficiency, preserving a flavorful moment in time.

Spiced Carrot Pickles

- **P.T.:** 30 minutes
- **Procedure:** Slice carrots into sticks. Boil a mixture of vinegar, water, sugar, and pickling spices. Pour over carrots in jars. Seal and refrigerate after cooling.
- **Ingr.:** 2 lb. carrots, peeled and sliced into sticks; 1 Cup vinegar; 1 Cup water; 1/2 Cups sugar; 1 Tblsp pickling spices.
- **Handling and Storage:** Refrigerate and consume within a month.

Sweet and Tangy Red Onion Pickles

- **P.T.:** 25 minutes
- **Procedure:** Thinly slice red onions. Combine vinegar, water, sugar, and salt. Bring to a boil and pour over onions in jars. Let cool, then seal and refrigerate.
- **Ingr.:** 3 large red onions, thinly sliced; 1 Cup vinegar; 1 Cup water; 1/2 Cups sugar; 1 Tblsp salt.
- **Handling and Storage:** Keep refrigerated and use within 3 weeks.

Garlic Dill Green Beans

- **P.T.:** 40 minutes
- **Procedure:** Trim green beans. Boil a mixture of vinegar, water, salt, dill, and garlic. Place beans in jars and cover with hot liquid. Seal after cooling and refrigerate.
- **Ingr.:** 1 lb. green beans, trimmed; 1 Cup vinegar; 1 Cup water; 2 tsp salt; 2 Tblsp fresh dill, chopped; 4 cloves garlic, minced.
- **Handling and Storage:** Refrigerate; best after 1 week, consume within a month.

Asian-Style Pickled Mushrooms

- **P.T.:** 35 minutes
- **Procedure:** Quarter mushrooms. Make a brine with soy sauce, vinegar, water, sugar, and ginger. Boil and pour over mushrooms. Cool, seal, and refrigerate.
- **Ingr.:** 1 lb. mushrooms, quartered; 1/2 Cups soy sauce; 1/2 Cups vinegar; 1/2 Cups water; 1/4 Cups sugar; 1 Tblsp fresh ginger, grated.
- **Handling and Storage:** Store in the refrigerator, consume within 3 weeks.

Pickled Beets with Cinnamon

- **P.T.:** 45 minutes

- **Procedure:** Roast and slice beets. Boil vinegar, water, sugar, cinnamon, and cloves. Pour over beets in jars. Let cool, then seal and refrigerate.
- **Ingr.:** 2 lb. beets, roasted and sliced; 1 Cup vinegar; 1 Cup water; 1/2 Cups sugar; 1 tsp cinnamon; 1/4 tsp cloves.
- **Handling and Storage:** Refrigerate and consume within a month.

Sweet Chili Cauliflower Pickles

- **P.T.:** 30 minutes
- **Procedure:** Break cauliflower into florets. Boil vinegar, water, sugar, and chili flakes. Pour over cauliflower. Cool, seal, and refrigerate.

- **Ingr.:** 1 head cauliflower, broken into florets; 1 Cup vinegar; 1 Cup water; 1/2 Cups sugar; 1 tsp chili flakes.
- **Handling and Storage:** Refrigerate and consume within a month.

Fiery Jalapeño Pickles

- **P.T.:** 20 minutes
- **Procedure:** Slice jalapeños. Boil vinegar, water, sugar, and garlic. Pour over jalapeños in jars. Let cool, then seal and refrigerate.
- **Ingr.:** 1 lb. jalapeños, sliced; 1 Cup vinegar; 1 Cup water; 1/2 Cups sugar 2 cloves garlic, minced.
- **Handling and Storage:** Store in the refrigerator, consume within 2 weeks.

Pickled Rainbow Peppers

- **P.T.:** 30 minutes
- **Procedure:** Slice bell peppers. Boil vinegar, water, sugar, and mustard seeds. Pour over peppers in jars. Cool, seal, and refrigerate.
- **Ingr.:** 2 lb. bell peppers, mixed colors, sliced; 1 Cup vinegar; 1 Cup water; 1/2 Cups sugar; 1 Tblsp mustard seeds.
- **Handling and Storage:** Refrigerate; best after 1 week, consume within a month.

Ginger-Pickled Daikon Radish

- **P.T.:** 25 minutes
- **Procedure:** Slice daikon radish. Make a brine with vinegar, water, sugar, and sliced ginger. Boil and pour over daikon. Cool, then seal and refrigerate.

- **Ingr.:** 1 large daikon radish, sliced; 1 Cup vinegar; 1 Cup water; 1/2 Cups sugar; 2 Tblsp fresh ginger, sliced.
- **Handling and Storage:** Keep refrigerated, consume within a month.

Pickled Cherry Tomatoes

- **P.T.:** 30 minutes
- **Procedure:** Pierce cherry tomatoes with a toothpick. Boil a mixture of white vinegar, water, sugar, and herbs. Pour over tomatoes in jars. Cool, seal, and refrigerate.

- **Ingr.:** 2 lb. cherry tomatoes, pierced with a toothpick; 1 Cup white vinegar; 1 Cup water; 1/2 Cups sugar; 1 Tblsp mixed herbs (thyme, oregano).
- **Handling and Storage:** Store in the refrigerator and consume within 4 weeks.

Spicy Pickled Okra

- **P.T.:** 40 minutes
- **Procedure:** Pack okra, garlic cloves, and a slice of lemon into jars. Boil vinegar, water, salt, and spices (cayenne pepper, dill seeds). Pour over okra. Seal after cooling and refrigerate.
- **Ingr.:** 2 lb. okra; 2 cloves garlic; 1 slice lemon; 1 Cup vinegar; 1 Cup water; 1 Tblsp salt; 1 tsp cayenne pepper; 1 tsp dill seeds.
- **Handling and Storage:** Refrigerate and consume within 6 weeks.

Sweet Pickled Red Cabbage

- **P.T.:** 35 minutes
- **Procedure:** Shred red cabbage. Boil a mixture of apple cider vinegar, water, sugar, and spices (cloves, cinnamon). Pour over cabbage. Seal after cooling and refrigerate.
- **Ingr.:** 1 head red cabbage, shredded; 1 Cup apple cider vinegar; 1 Cup water; 1/2 Cups sugar; 1 tsp cloves; 1 cinnamon stick.
- **Handling and Storage:** Keep refrigerated and use within 2 months.

Pickled Asparagus Spears

- **P.T.:** 30 minutes
- **Procedure:** Pack asparagus spears into jars with dill and garlic. Boil vinegar, water, and salt. Pour over asparagus. Seal and refrigerate after cooling.
- **Ingr.:** 2 lb. asparagus, trimmed; 2 cloves garlic; 2 Tblsp dill; 1 Cup vinegar; 1 Cup water; 2 tsp salt.
- **Handling and Storage:** Refrigerate and consume within 6 weeks.

Pickled Ginger (Gari)

- **P.T.:** 45 minutes
- **Procedure:** Thinly slice young ginger. Sprinkle with salt and let sit for 30 minutes. Boil a mixture of rice vinegar and sugar. Pour over ginger slices. Seal and refrigerate.
- **Ingr.:** 1/2 lb. young ginger, peeled and thinly sliced; 1/2 Cups rice vinegar; 1/4 Cups sugar; 1 tsp salt.
- **Handling and Storage:** Store in the refrigerator and consume within 2 months.

Pickled Pearl Onions

- **P.T.:** 40 minutes
- **Procedure:** Peel pearl onions. Boil a mixture of vinegar, water, sugar, and spices (bay leaves, peppercorns). Pour over onions in jars. Cool, seal, and refrigerate.
- **Ingr.:** 1 lb. pearl onions, peeled; 1 Cup vinegar; 1 Cup water; 1/2 Cups sugar 2 bay leaves; 1 tsp peppercorns.
- **Handling and Storage:** Refrigerate and consume within 6 weeks.

Pickled Yellow Squash

- **P.T.:** 30 minutes
- **Procedure:** Slice yellow squash thinly. Boil vinegar, water, sugar, and mustard seeds. Pour over squash in jars. Seal and refrigerate after cooling.
- **Ingr.:** 2 lb. yellow squash, thinly sliced; 1 Cup vinegar; 1 Cup water; 1/2 Cups sugar; 1 Tblsp mustard seeds.
- **Handling and Storage:** Keep refrigerated and use within a month.

Pickled Radishes with Peppercorns

- **P.T.:** 25 minutes
- **Procedure:** Slice radishes thinly. Boil white vinegar, water, sugar, and whole peppercorns. Pour over radishes. Cool, seal, and refrigerate.
- **Ingr.:** 1 lb. radishes, thinly sliced; 1 Cup white vinegar; 1 Cup water; 1/2 Cups sugar; 1 Tblsp whole peppercorns.
- **Handling and Storage:** Store in the refrigerator, consume within a month.

Pickled Green Peppers

- **P.T.:** 30 minutes
- **Procedure:** Slice green peppers into strips. Boil vinegar, water, salt, and garlic. Pour over peppers in jars. Cool, then seal and refrigerate.
- **Ingr.:** 2 lb. green peppers, sliced into strips; 1 Cup vinegar; 1 Cup water; 2 tsp salt; 2 cloves garlic, minced.
- **Handling and Storage:** Refrigerate and consume within 4 weeks.

Curried Pickled Cauliflower

- **P.T.:** 40 minutes
- **Procedure:** Break cauliflower into small florets. Boil vinegar, water, sugar, curry powder, and turmeric. Pour over cauliflower. Seal after cooling and refrigerate.
- **Ingr.:** 1 head cauliflower, broken into small florets; 1 Cup vinegar; 1 Cup water; 1/2 Cups sugar; 1 Tblsp curry powder; 1 tsp turmeric.
- **Handling and Storage:** Keep refrigerated and use within 6 weeks.

Pickled Fennel with Citrus

- **P.T.:** 35 minutes
- **Procedure:** Slice fennel bulbs thinly. Boil a mix of white wine vinegar, water, sugar, lemon zest, and orange zest. Pour over fennel. Cool, seal, and refrigerate.
- **Ingr.:** 2 fennel bulbs, thinl sliced; 1 Cup white wine vinegar; 1 Cup water; 1/2 Cups sugar; 1 Tblsp lemon zest; 1 Tblsp orange zest.
- **Handling and Storage:** Store in the refrigerator an consume within a month.

Smoking and Curing Meats: Traditional and Modern Methods

Smoking and curing meat are ancient techniques that transform raw cuts into flavorful, preserved delicacies. These methods, rooted in tradition, are ideal for preparing bacon, ham, jerky, and sausages. By using salt, sugar, and smoke, these processes not only enhance the meat's flavor but also extend its shelf life, creating a perfect balance of taste and preservation.

The principles behind smoking and curing are straightforward: salt and smoke inhibit the growth of harmful microorganisms. During curing, salt draws out moisture from the meat, creating an environment where bacteria struggle to survive. Smoking further enhances this effect by adding a layer of antimicrobial compounds and infusing the meat with rich, smoky flavors. These combined techniques ensure that the meat remains safe to eat for extended periods.

The journey begins with selecting high-quality cuts of meat. Pork bellies for bacon, hams for curing, and lean beef for jerky are chosen with care, as the quality of the final product depends largely on the initial ingredients. This selection is critical, ensuring that only the best cuts undergo the meticulous process of curing and smoking.

Preparation involves a precise blend of salt, sugar, and spices. The meat is rubbed or submerged in this curing mixture, allowing the salt to penetrate deeply, drawing out moisture and infusing flavor. This stage, often taking days or even weeks, is essential for developing the meat's distinctive taste and texture. Herbs and spices are added to enhance the flavor profile, creating a unique signature for each batch.

Smoking is the next crucial step. The cured meat is exposed to smoke from burning wood, typically hardwoods like oak, hickory, or applewood, which impart different flavor notes. The smoking process can be cold or hot, depending on the desired outcome. Cold smoking adds flavor without cooking the meat, while hot smoking cooks the meat as it smokes, ensuring it is ready to eat.

As the smoke envelops the meat, a transformation occurs. The smoke's heat and chemical compounds work together to further preserve and flavor the meat. Timing and temperature control are critical, as too much or too little smoke can affect the final product. The art of smoking lies in achieving the perfect balance, ensuring that the meat is infused with just the right amount of smoky goodness.

Once the smoking process is complete, the meat is left to rest and mature. This resting period allows the flavors to meld and deepen, resulting in a product that is rich in taste and complexity. Proper storage in a cool, dry place ensures that the meat remains safe and flavorful for months.

Each piece of smoked and cured meat is a testament to these time-honored techniques. From the first bite of a smoky, savory jerky to the rich, salty taste of cured ham, these methods celebrate the art of preservation and the joy of flavor. Smoking and curing meat are not just culinary practices; they are a connection to our past, a way of savoring and safeguarding the harvest, and a tribute to the ingenuity of food preservation.

Classic Smoked Brisket

- **P.T.:** 12 hours (including marinating)
- **Procedure:** Marinate a beef brisket with a blend of salt, black pepper, and garlic powder overnight. Smoke at 225°F for about 8 hours or until tender.
- **Ingr.:** 1 whole beef brisket (5-6 lb.); 3 Tblsp salt; 3 Tblsp black pepper; 1 Tblsp garlic powder.
- **Handling and Storage:** Consume within 3 days if refrigerated, or slice and freeze for longer storage.

Applewood Smoked Chicken

- **P.T.:** 4 hours (including marinating)
- **Procedure:** Brine chicken in a solution of water, salt, sugar, and herbs for 2 hours. Smoke with applewood chips at 250°F until the internal temperature reaches 165°F.
- **Ingr.:** 1 whole chicken (4- lb.); 4 Cups water; 1/4 Cups salt; 1/4 Cups sugar; 2 Tblsp mixed herbs (thyme, rosemary).
- **Handling and Storage:** Refrigerate and consume within 3 days, or freeze.

Hickory-Smoked Pork Ribs

- **P.T.:** 6 hours

- **Procedure:** Rub pork ribs with a mixture of paprika, brown sugar, and spices. Smoke over hickory wood at 225°F for about 5 hours, applying a barbecue glaze in the final hour.

- **Ingr.:** 2 racks pork ribs (about 4 lb. total); 2 Tblsp paprika; 1/4 Cups brown sugar; 1 Tblsp garlic powder; 1 Tblsp onion powder; 1 tsp cayenne pepper; 1/2 Cups barbecue glaze.
- **Handling and Storage:** Best consumed immediately; store leftovers in the refrigerator for up to 3 days.

Maple-Cured Bacon

- **P.T.:** 7 days (curing time)
- **Procedure:** Cure pork belly in a mixture of kosher salt, maple syrup, and curing salt for 7 days. Rinse and smoke at 200°F until the internal temperature reaches 150°F.

- **Ingr.:** 5 lb. pork belly; 1/4 Cups kosher salt; 1/4 Cups maple syrup; 2 tsp curing salt.
- **Handling and Storage:** Slice and refrigerate for up to 2 weeks, or freeze.

Cold-Smoked Salmon

- **P.T.:** 48 hours (including curing)

- **Procedure:** Cure salmon in a mix of salt, sugar, and dill for 36 hours. Rinse, dry, and cold smoke at 80°F for 12 hours.
- **Ingr.:** 2 lb. salmon fillet; 1/2 Cups salt; 1/2 Cups sugar; 1/4 Cups chopped dill.
- **Handling and Storage:** Slice thinly; refrigerate and consume within 1 week.

Smoked Beef Jerky

- **P.T.:** 24 hours (including marinating)
- **Procedure:** Marinate thin strips of beef in a mixture of soy sauce, Worcestershire sauce, and spices. Smoke at 160°F until dry and leathery.

- **Ingr.:** 2 lb. beef (lean cuts); 1/2 Cups soy sauce; 1/4 Cups Worcestershire sauce; 1 Tblsp garlic powder; 1 tsp black pepper; 1 tsp onion powde
- **Handling and Storage:** Store in an airtight container at room temperature for up to 1 month.

Smoked Gouda Cheese

- **P.T.:** 4 hours
- **Procedure:** Cold smoke Gouda cheese at 90°F for 3 hours, turning occasionally. Wrap in parchment paper and age in the refrigerator for at least one week.
- **Ingr.:** 1 lb. Gouda cheese.
- **Handling and Storage:** Keep refrigerated; consume within 2 months.

Peppercorn-Crusted Smoked Duck

- **P.T.:** 5 hours
- **Procedure:** Cure duck breasts in a mixture of salt, sugar, and crushed peppercorns for 4 hours. Rinse, dry, and smoke at 225°F until the internal temperature reaches 160°F.
- **Ingr.:** 2 duck breasts; 1/4 Cups salt; 1/4 Cups sugar; 2 Tblsp crushed black peppercorns.
- **Handling and Storage:** Refrigerate and consume within 4 days, or freeze.

Country-Style Smoked Sausages

- **P.T.:** 8 hours (including resting)
- **Procedure:** Prepare sausage mixture with ground pork, spices, and curing salt. Stuff into casings and leave to rest overnight. Smoke at 225°F for 3 hours.
- **Ingr.:** 3 lb. ground pork; 1 Tblsp salt; 1 Tblsp paprika; 1 tsp curing salt; Casings for stuffing.
- **Handling and Storage:** Refrigerate and consume within a week, or freeze.

Apple Cider Cured Ham

- **P.T.:** 5 days (curing time)
- **Procedure:** Submerge ham in a brine of apple cider, kosher salt, brown sugar, and curing salt for 5 days. Rinse, dry, and smoke at 225°F until the internal temperature reaches 145°F.
- **Ingr.:** 1 whole ham (8-10 lb.); 4 Cups apple cider; 1 Cup kosher salt; 1 Cup brown sugar; 2 tsp curing salt.
- **Handling and Storage:** Slice and refrigerate for up to 10 days, or freeze.

Smoked Turkey Legs

- **P.T.:** 6 hours (including brining)
- **Procedure:** Brine turkey legs in a solution of water, salt, and brown sugar for 4 hours. Smoke over cherry wood at 225°F until the internal temperature reaches 165°F.
- **Ingr.:** 4 turkey legs; 4 Cups water; 1/4 Cups salt; 1/4 Cups brown sugar.
- **Handling and Storage:** Best consumed immediately; refrigerate leftovers for up to 3 days.

Spiced Pastrami

- **P.T.:** 5 days (curing time)
- **Procedure:** Cure beef brisket in a mix of curing salt, sugar, and pickling spices for 5 days. Rinse, coat with a blend of coriander and black pepper, and smoke at 225°F until the internal temperature reaches 190°F.
- **Ingr.:** 1 beef brisket (4-5 lb.); 1/4 Cups curing salt; 1/4 Cups sugar; 2 Tblsp pickling spices; 2 Tblsp ground coriander; 2 Tblsp cracked black pepper.
- **Handling and Storage:** Slice and refrigerate for up to 2 weeks.

Garlic and Herb Smoked Pork Loin

- **P.T.:** 3 hours
- **Procedure:** Rub a pork loin with a mix of garlic, rosemary, thyme, and olive oil. Smoke at 225°F until the internal temperature reaches 145°F.
- **Ingr.:** 1 pork loin (3-4 lb.), 2 Tblsp minced garlic; 1 Tblsp rosemary; 1 Tblsp thyme; 2 Tblsp olive oil.
- **Handling and Storage:** Refrigerate and consume within 5 days.

Maple Smoked Bacon

- **P.T.:** 7 days (curing time)
- **Procedure:** Cure pork belly in a mix of kosher salt, maple syrup, and pink curing salt for 7 days. Rinse, dry, and smoke at 200°F until the internal temperature reaches 150°F.
- **Ingr.:** 5 lb. pork belly; 1/4 Cups kosher salt; 1/4 Cups maple syrup; 2 tsp pink curing salt.
- **Handling and Storage:** Slice, refrigerate, and use within 2 weeks.

Hickory Smoked Venison Jerky

- **P.T.:** 24 hours (including marinating)
- **Procedure:** Slice venison into thin strips. Marinate in a mixture of soy sauce, Worcestershire sauce, and spices. Smoke at 165°F until dry.
- **Ingr.:** 2 lb. venison; 1/2 Cups soy sauce; 1/4 Cups Worcestershire sauce; 1 Tblsp garlic powder; 1 tsp black pepper; 1 tsp onion powder.
- **Handling and Storage:** Store in an airtight container for up to 1 month.

Smoked Duck Breast

- **P.T.:** 4 hours
- **Procedure:** Cure duck breasts with a mix of salt and sugar for 2 hours. Rinse and smoke at 225°F until the internal temperature reaches 160°F.
- **Ingr.:** 2 duck breasts; 1/4 Cups salt; 1/4 Cups sugar.
- **Handling and Storage:** Best consumed immediately; refrigerate leftovers for up to 3 days.

Smoked Andouille Sausage

- **P.T.:** 8 hours (including resting)
- **Procedure:** Prepare sausage mixture with ground pork, garlic, and Cajun spices. Stuff into casings and rest overnight. Smoke at 225°F for 3 hours.
- **Ingr.:** 3 lb. ground pork; 2 Tblsp minced garlic; 2 Tbls Cajun spices; Casings for stuffing.
- **Handling and Storage:** Refrigerate and consume within 1 week, or freeze.

Cured and Smoked Lamb Ribs

- **P.T.:** 3 days (curing time)
- **Procedure:** Cure lamb ribs in a mixture of salt, sugar, and rosemary for 3 days. Rinse, dry, and smoke at 225°F until tender.
- **Ingr.:** 2 lb. lamb ribs; 1/4 Cups salt; 1/4 Cups sugar; 1 Tblsp chopped rosemary.
- **Handling and Storage:** Best consumed immediately; refrigerate leftovers for up to 4 days.

Cold Smoked Cheese

- **P.T.:** 4 hours

- **Procedure:** Cold smoke cheeses like cheddar or gouda at 90°F for 2-3 hours, turning occasionally. Wrap in parchment paper and age in the refrigerator for at least one week.
- **Ingr.:** 1 lb. cheese (cheddar or gouda).
- **Handling and Storage:** Keep refrigerated; consume within 2 months.

Smoked Trout

- **P.T.:** 6 hours (including brining)
- **Procedure:** Brine trout in a solution of water, salt, and sugar for 2 hours. Smoke over applewood at 175°F until the fish is flaky.

- **Ingr.:** 2 lb. trout; 4 Cups water; 1/4 Cups salt; 1/4 Cups sugar.
- **Handling and Storage:** Best consumed immediately; refrigerate leftovers for up to 3 days.

Book V: Advanced Preservation and Storage

Building a Varied and Nutritious Prepper's Pantry

Embarking on this path, one must first envision a repository far beyond the realm of basic staples. It's a thoughtful curation of various foods, each selected for its nutritional value, shelf life, and role in enriching your diet. Imagine shelves adorned with jars of fruits, capturing their peak sweetness, alongside a rainbow of vegetables, each offering its unique blend of vitamins and minerals. The section for proteins, preserved through canning or drying, forms a robust foundation for nutritious meals. The soul of this endeavor lies in striking a balance between dietary richness and flavor. This equilibrium is achieved through an eclectic mix of preservation techniques. Canning, for instance, seals in the freshness and essence of fruits and vegetables, while dehydration concentrates and intensifies flavors in meats, preserving their vital proteins. Fermentation, a time-honored ally, not only elongates shelf life but also enriches foods with gut-friendly probiotics, enhancing both taste and health benefits.

Aligning with nature's cycles, this storage system reflects the bounty of the seasons. It's a celebration of the year's rhythm, from the lushness of summer berries to the heartiness of autumn's squashes, the sturdiness of winter root vegetables, and the tender offerings of spring. This seasonal approach not only ensures a rotating variety of nutrients but also maintains a connection with the natural availability of produce, often yielding better flavors and more potent nutrition.

Integrating flavors from around the globe adds another layer of excitement to this culinary treasury. Elements like the tang of kimchi, the sweet allure of mango chutney, or the robust depth of a Mediterranean olive tapenade transform simple meals into global culinary experiences, right from the comfort of your home.

In constructing this collection, the focus on both quantity and quality is paramount. It's essential to not only stockpile but also curate a selection that maintains its integrity and nutritional value over time. Regular inspection, rotation, and adherence to preservation standards are vital in ensuring each item remains ready to fulfill its intended purpose.

The transformation of these stored goods into meals represents the culmination of this process. Each ingredient, each preserved item, becomes an actor in the culinary stories you craft. This aspect of cooking evolves into an adventure, a delightful journey through flavors and textures, all sourced from the security and abundance of your own provisions.

In the process of assembling this collection, ethical considerations play a significant role. Opting for sustainable sources, supporting local growers, and choosing organic options not only contribute to environmental stewardship but also amplify the health benefits of the foods you store. This ethical approach speaks to a larger commitment, one that encompasses personal health and the well-being of our planet.

Long-Term Storage Techniques: Vacuum Sealing, Freezing, and More

Moving forward from the establishment of a varied and nutritious cache, we delve into the nuances of long-term storage techniques. This facet of food preservation i pivotal in ensuring the longevity and safety of your provisions, playing a critical rol in upholding the essence of a self-reliant lifestyle.

Vacuum sealing emerges as a modern marvel in the preservation landscape. Thi method involves extracting air from the package, thereby significantly reducing th presence of oxygen – a key factor in the deterioration of food. The benefits of vacuur sealing are manifold. Not only does it extend the shelf life of foods by preventing th growth of aerobic bacteria and fungi, but it also retains the food's texture, moistur content, and flavor. This technique is particularly effective for dry goods, such a grains and legumes, as well as for meats and cheeses, safeguarding them agains freezer burn when stored in a frozen state.

Freezing, a time-honored method, continues to be a reliable ally in long-term foo preservation. Its simplicity and effectiveness cannot be overstated. When don correctly, freezing preserves the nutritional value, texture, and taste of foods. Th key here is to understand the proper techniques of blanching and pre-freezing especially for fruits and vegetables. Blanching, a brief immersion in boiling wate followed by a plunge into ice water, halts the enzymatic activity that can degrade th quality of food over time. Pre-freezing individual pieces on a tray before transferrin them to airtight containers or bags prevents clumping, ensuring easy access an portion control.

In addition to these methods, there's an array of techniques to consider fo specialized items. Herbs, for instance, can be frozen in olive oil in ice cube trays offering convenient, flavor-packed portions for cooking. Liquid-based foods, like soup and sauces, can be frozen in silicone molds or containers, providing a hassle-fre solution for quick meals. The key to effective freezing lies in meticulous labeling an regular rotation, ensuring that older items are used first and nothing is lost to freeze burn or forgotten in the recesses of the freezer.

Furthermore, the art of canning itself, a topic covered in previous chapters, plays a significant role in long-term storage. However, the focus here shifts to bulk preparation strategies. Seasonal harvests, bulk purchases, or a particularly successful hunting or fishing trip can yield a substantial amount of perishable food that needs to be preserved swiftly. In these instances, efficient batch processing, careful planning, and adherence to safety protocols are paramount. This approach not only ensures a steady supply of food but also capitalizes on the economic and logistical advantages of bulk preservation.

As we consider these varied techniques, it's important to note that each method has its specific applications and advantages. The choice of technique will depend on the type of food, available storage space, and personal preferences. The ultimate goal is to create a comprehensive system that combines these methods harmoniously, ensuring that your provisions are not only safe and nutritious but also diverse and appealing.

Seasonal and Bulk Canning: Strategies for Year-Round Preparation

Seasonal canning aligns with the natural ebb and flow of produce availability. It involves a strategic approach to harvesting and preserving fruits and vegetables at their peak freshness. This method not only maximizes the nutritional and flavor profiles of the produce but also allows for a varied diet throughout the year. The key here is anticipation and preparation. As each season approaches, planning which crops to focus on, understanding their peak harvest times, and preparing the necessary canning supplies in advance are essential steps. This proactive approach transforms the seasonal harvest into a rhythm of preservation, seamlessly integrating it into your routine.

When dealing with bulk canning, the approach shifts to efficiency and scalability. Bulk canning often occurs when dealing with large quantities of produce, either from personal garden, community share, or a bulk purchase. The challenge here lies in managing the volume of food without compromising on safety or quality. Implementing batch processing techniques, organizing workspace and workflow, and ensuring that all equipment is in optimal condition are vital components. This might involve setting up multiple canning stations, scheduling different stages of the canning process, and enlisting help to manage the workload effectively.

One of the critical aspects of seasonal and bulk canning is understanding the variations in preparation and processing times for different types of produce. For instance, fruits typically require a different treatment than vegetables, and high-acid foods have different canning requirements compared to low-acid ones. Adapting your methods to suit these variations is crucial for the success of your preservation efforts. Another important consideration is the storage and rotation of canned goods. Proper labeling with dates and contents, organizing the storage space to facilitate easy access and rotation, and regular inspection for spoilage or seal failure are practices that ensure the longevity and safety of your canned goods. These practices not only help in maintaining a well-organized pantry but also in reducing waste and ensuring continuous supply of high-quality food.

Additionally, embracing creativity in your canning recipes can add a delightful twist to the process. Experimenting with flavors, trying out new combinations, and even incorporating international canning recipes can make the process enjoyable and the results rewarding. This creative exploration not only enhances the variety in your pantry but also keeps the practice of canning exciting and engaging.

Book VI: Special Topics and Recipes

Special Dietary Considerations: Low-Sugar, Low-Salt, and Allergen-Free Recipes

Golden Harvest Apple Butter

- **P.T.:** 1 hour
- **Acidity level:** Moderate
- **Head Space:** 1/4 inch
- **Jar and Lid Preparation:** Sterilize jars and lids
- **Procedure:** Combine sliced apples, water, and a dash of cinnamon in a pot. Simmer until apples are tender. Puree the mixture and return to pot. Add lemon juice and a touch of honey. Cook until thickened.

- **Ingr.:** 5 lb. apples, peeled, cored, and sliced; 1 Cup water; 1 tsp cinnamon; 1/4 Cups lemon juice; 1/2 Cups honey.
- **Handling and Storage Instructions:** Process in a water bath for 10 minutes. Store in a cool, dark place.

Summer Zucchini Relish

- **P.T.:** 45 minutes
- **Acidity level:** High
- **Head Space:** 1/2 inch
- **Jar and Lid Preparation:** Sterilize jars and lids
- **Procedure:** Combine grated zucchini, onions, red bell pepper, and apple cider vinegar in a large pot. Add mustard seeds, turmeric, and a pinch of stevia. Simmer until thick.

- **Ingr.:** 2 lb. zucchini, grated; 1 large onion, chopped; 1 red bell pepper, chopped; 2 Cups apple cider vinegar; 1 Tblsp mustard seeds; 1 tsp turmeric; 1/4 Cups stevia.
- **Handling and Storage Instructions:** Process in a water bath for 15 minutes. Keep in a cool, dark place.

Rustic Pear Preserve

- **P.T.:** 1.5 hours
- **Acidity level:** Moderate
- **Head Space:** 1/4 inch
- **Jar and Lid Preparation:** Sterilize jars and lids
- **Procedure:** Simmer diced pears with a hint of vanilla and maple syrup. Stir in pectin and lemon juice until thickened.
- **Ingr.:** 4 lb. pears, peeled and diced; 1 tsp vanilla extract; 1/2 Cups maple syrup; 1 package pectin; 1/4 Cups lemon juice.
- **Handling and Storage Instructions:** Process in a water bath for 10 minutes. Store in a cool, dark place.

Garden Veggie Salsa

- **P.T.:** 30 minutes
- **Acidity level:** High
- **Head Space:** 1/2 inch
- **Jar and Lid Preparation:** Sterilize jars and lids
- **Procedure:** Mix chopped tomatoes, green peppers, onions, and a jalapeño. Add lime juice, cilantro, and a sprinkle of sea salt. Simmer until flavors meld.
- **Ingr.:** 3 large tomatoes, chopped; 2 green peppers, chopped; 1 large onion, chopped 1 jalapeño, chopped; 1/4 Cups lime juice; 1/4 Cups cilantro, minced; 1 tsp sea salt.
- **Handling and Storage Instructions:** Process in a water bath for 15 minutes. Store in a cool, dark place.

Tangy Cranberry Sauce

- **P.T.:** 30 minutes
- **Acidity level:** High
- **Head Space:** 1/4 inch
- **Jar and Lid Preparation:** Sterilize jars and lids
- **Procedure:** Cook cranberries with orange zest and juice. Add a bit of maple syrup for sweetness. Boil until berries pop and sauce thickens.
- **Ingr.:** 4 Cups cranberries; 1 orange, zest and juice; 1/2 Cups maple syrup.
- **Handling and Storage Instructions:** Process in a water bath for 10 minutes. Store in a cool, dark place.

Roasted Red Pepper Spread

- **P.T.:** 1 hour
- **Acidity level:** Moderate
- **Head Space:** 1/2 inch
- **Jar and Lid Preparation:** Sterilize jars and lids
- **Procedure:** Roast red peppers, blend with garlic, balsamic vinegar, and a hint of basil. Simmer until it reaches a spreadable consistency.
- **Ingr.:** 4 large red peppers, roasted; 2 cloves garlic, minced; 1/4 Cups balsamic vinegar; 1 Tblsp basil, minced.
- **Handling and Storage Instructions:** Process in a water bath for 15 minutes. Store in a cool, dark place.

Savory Mushroom Pâté

- **P.T.:** 1 hour
- **Acidity level:** Low
- **Head Space:** 1/2 inch
- **Jar and Lid Preparation:** Sterilize jars and lids
- **Procedure:** Sauté mushrooms with onions, thyme, and a splash of soy sauce. Blend into a smooth pâté. Simmer until thickened.
- **Ingr.:** 1 lb. mushrooms, chopped; 1 large onion, chopped; 1 Tblsp thyme, minced; 2 Tblsp soy sauce.
- **Handling and Storage Instructions:** Process in a pressure canner for 75 minutes. Store in a cool, dark place.

Cinnamon Apple Chutney

- **P.T.:** 1 hour
- **Acidity level:** Moderate
- **Head Space:** 1/2 inch
- **Jar and Lid Preparation:** Sterilize jars and lids
- **Procedure:** Cook diced apples with raisins, cinnamon, and a splash of apple cider vinegar. Stir in a bit of honey and ginger until thickened.
- **Ingr.:** 4 lb. apples, diced; 1 Cup raisins; 1 tsp cinnamon; 1/4 Cup apple cider vinegar; 1/2 Cups honey; 1 Tblsp ginger, minced.
- **Handling and Storage Instructions:** Process in a water bath for 15 minutes. Store in a cool, dark place.

Balsamic Onion Marmalade

- **P.T.:** 1 hour
- **Acidity level:** Moderate
- **Head Space:** 1/4 inch
- **Jar and Lid Preparation:** Sterilize jars and lids
- **Procedure:** Caramelize onions, then simmer with balsamic vinegar and a touch of brown sugar. Cook until it reaches a marmalade consistency.
- **Ingr.:** 5 large onions, thinly sliced; 1/2 Cups balsamic vinegar; 1/4 Cups brown sugar.
- **Handling and Storage Instructions:** Process in a water bath for 10 minutes. Store in a cool, dark place.

Lemon-Thyme Jelly

- **P.T.:** 50 minutes
- **Acidity level:** High
- **Head Space:** 1/4 inch
- **Jar and Lid Preparation:** Sterilize jars and lids
- **Procedure:** Combine fresh lemon juice with a hint of thyme and a substitute sweetener like xylitol. Add pectin and simmer until it gels.
- **Ingr.:** 1 Cup lemon juice; 1 Tblsp thyme, finely chopped; 1 Cup xylitol; 1 package pectin.
- **Handling and Storage Instructions:** Process in a water bath for 10 minutes. Store in a cool, dark location.

Beetroot and Ginger Chutney

- **P.T.:** 1.5 hours
- **Acidity level:** Moderate
- **Head Space:** 1/2 inch
- **Jar and Lid Preparation:** Sterilize jars and lids
- **Procedure:** Roast beets and blend with fresh ginger, apple cider vinegar, and a touch of honey. Simmer until thickened.
- **Ingr.:** 3 large beetroots, roasted and peeled; 1 Tblsp ginger, minced; 1/4 Cups apple cider vinegar; 1/4 Cups honey.
- **Handling and Storage Instructions:** Process in a water bath for 15 minutes. Keep in a cool, dark place.

Spicy Green Tomato Salsa

- **P.T.:** 40 minutes
- **Acidity level:** High
- **Head Space:** 1/2 inch
- **Jar and Lid Preparation:** Sterilize jars and lids
- **Procedure:** Combine chopped green tomatoes, jalapenos, onions, and lime juice. Season with cilantro and a pinch of salt. Cook until flavors blend.
- **Ingr.:** 2 lb. green tomatoes, chopped; 2 jalapenos, chopped; large onion, chopped; 1/4 Cups lime juice; 1/4 Cups cilantro, minced; 1 tsp salt.
- **Handling and Storage Instructions:** Process in a water bath for 15 minutes. Store in a cool, dark area.

Carrot and Orange Marmalade

- **P.T.:** 1 hour
- **Acidity level:** Moderate
- **Head Space:** 1/4 inch
- **Jar and Lid Preparation:** Sterilize jars and lids
- **Procedure:** Simmer grated carrots and orange zest with a splash of orange juice and a sugar substitute. Add pectin and cook until it thickens.
- **Ingr.:** 2 lb. carrots, grated; 2 oranges, zest and juice; 1/4 Cups orange juice; 1 package pectin; 1/4 Cups sugar substitute.
- **Handling and Storage Instructions:** Process in a water bath for 10 minutes. Store in a cool, dark location.

Minted Pea Spread

- **P.T.:** 35 minutes
- **Acidity level:** Low
- **Head Space:** 1/2 inch
- **Jar and Lid Preparation:** Sterilize jars and lids
- **Procedure:** Blend cooked peas with fresh mint, a splash of lemon juice, and a hint of garlic. Simmer until it reaches a spreadable consistency.
- **Ingr.:** 2 Cups peas, cooked; 1/4 Cups mint, minced; 2 Tblsp lemon juice; 1 clove garlic, minced.
- **Handling and Storage Instructions:** Process in a pressure canner for 75 minutes. Store in a cool, dark place.

Pickled Rainbow Chard Stems

- **P.T.:** 30 minutes
- **Acidity level:** High
- **Head Space:** 1/2 inch
- **Jar and Lid Preparation:** Sterilize jars and lids
- **Procedure:** Brine chard stems in a mixture of vinegar, water, and a bit of sweetener. Add mustard seeds and garlic for flavor. Boil until stems are tender.
- **Ingr.:** 1 lb. chard stems, trimmed; 1 Cup vinegar; 1 Cup water; 1 Tblsp sugar substitute; Tblsp mustard seeds; 2 cloves garlic, minced.
- **Handling and Storage Instructions:** Process in a water bath for 10 minutes. Keep in a cool, dark place.

Raspberry and Rosewater Jam

- **P.T.:** 50 minutes
- **Acidity level:** Moderate
- **Head Space:** 1/4 inch
- **Jar and Lid Preparation:** Sterilize jars and lids
- **Procedure:** Cook raspberries with a splash of rosewater and a sugar substitute. Stir in pectin until it gels.
- **Ingr.:** 4 Cups raspberries; 1 tsp rosewater; 1 Cup sugar substitute; 1 package pectin.
- **Handling and Storage Instructions:** Process in a water bath for 10 minutes. Store in a cool, dark area.

Savory Pumpkin Butter

- **P.T.:** 1 hour
- **Acidity level:** Moderate
- **Head Space:** 1/4 inch
- **Jar and Lid Preparation:** Sterilize jars and lids
- **Procedure:** Blend roasted pumpkin with a hint of nutmeg, cinnamon, and a sugar substitute. Simmer until smooth and thick.
- **Ingr.:** 4 Cups pumpkin, roasted and pureed; 1 tsp nutmeg; 1 tsp cinnamon; 1/4 Cups sugar substitute.
- **Handling and Storage Instructions:** Process in a water bath for 10 minutes. Keep in a cool, dark place.

Sun-Dried Tomato Tapenade

- **P.T.:** 40 minutes
- **Acidity level:** Low
- **Head Space:** 1/2 inch
- **Jar and Lid Preparation:** Sterilize jars and lids
- **Procedure:** Blend sun-dried tomatoes with olives, capers, and a splash of olive oil. Add a touch of garlic and basil for flavor.
- **Ingr.:** 1 Cup sun-dried tomatoes; 1/2 Cups olives; 2 Tblsp capers; 1/4 Cups olive oil; 2 cloves garlic, minced; 1 Tblsp basil, minced.
- **Handling and Storage Instructions:** Process in a pressure canner for 75 minutes. Store in a cool, dark location.

Apple and Cranberry Chutney

- **P.T.:** 1 hour
- **Acidity level:** Moderate
- **Head Space:** 1/2 inch
- **Jar and Lid Preparation:** Sterilize jars and lids
- **Procedure:** Simmer chopped apples and cranberries with a hint of cinnamon and a sugar substitute. Add apple cider vinegar and cook until thickened.
- **Ingr.:** 3 lb. apples, chopped; 2 Cups cranberries; 1 tsp cinnamon; 1/4 Cups apple cider vinegar; 1/4 Cups sugar substitute.
- **Handling and Storage Instructions:** Process in a water bath for 15 minutes. Keep in a cool, dark area.

Garlic Dill Pickles

- **P.T.:** 45 minutes
- **Acidity level:** High
- **Head Space:** 1/2 inch
- **Jar and Lid Preparation:** Sterilize jars and lids
- **Procedure:** Soak cucumbers in a brine of vinegar, water, and a sugar substitute. Add fresh dill and garlic cloves. Simmer briefly before packing into jars.
- **Ingr.:** 2 lb. cucumbers, sliced; 2 Cups vinegar; 2 Cups water; 1/4 Cups sugar substitute; 1/4 Cups fresh dill, minced; 4 cloves garlic minced.
- **Handling and Storage Instructions:** Process in a water bath for 10 minutes. Store in a cool, dark place.

Strawberry Rhubarb Compote

- **P.T.:** 50 minutes
- **Acidity level:** Moderate
- **Head Space:** 1/4 inch
- **Jar and Lid Preparation:** Sterilize jars and lids
- **Procedure:** Combine strawberries and rhubarb with a sugar substitute and lemon juice. Cook until fruit softens and mixture thickens.
- **Ingr.:** 2 Cups strawberries, chopped; 2 Cups rhubarb, chopped; 1 Cup sugar substitute; 1/4 Cups lemon juice.
- **Handling and Storage Instructions:** Process in a water bath for 10 minutes. Store in a cool, dark place.

Pickled Red Onions

- **P.T.:** 30 minutes
- **Acidity level:** High
- **Head Space:** 1/2 inch
- **Jar and Lid Preparation:** Sterilize jars and lids
- **Procedure:** Slice red onions and pickle in a mixture of vinegar, water, and a pinch of sugar substitute. Add peppercorns and bay leaves for flavor.
- **Ingr.:** 3 large red onions, thinly sliced; 1 Cup vinegar; 1 Cup water; 1 Tblsp sugar substitute; 1 tsp peppercorns; 2 bay leaves.
- **Handling and Storage Instructions:** Process in a water bath for 10 minutes. Store in a cool, dark place.

Apricot Vanilla Spread

- **P.T.:** 1 hour
- **Acidity level:** Moderate
- **Head Space:** 1/4 inch
- **Jar and Lid Preparation:** Sterilize jars and lids
- **Procedure:** Cook apricots with vanilla extract and a sugar substitute. Stir in pectin and simmer until thick.
- **Ingr.:** 3 lb. apricots, chopped; 1 tsp vanilla extract; 1/4 Cups sugar substitute; 1 package pectin.
- **Handling and Storage Instructions:** Process in a water bath for 10 minutes. Store in a cool, dark place.

Basil Pesto

- **P.T.:** 30 minutes
- **Acidity level:** Low
- **Head Space:** 1/2 inch
- **Jar and Lid Preparation:** Sterilize jars and lids
- **Procedure:** Blend fresh basil leaves, pine nuts, garlic, and olive oil. Add a squeeze of lemon juice for freshness.
- **Ingr.:** 2 Cups basil leaves; 1/2 Cups pine nuts; 4 cloves garlic, minced; 1/2 Cups olive oil; 1 Tblsp lemon juice.
- **Handling and Storage Instructions:** Process in a pressure canner for 75 minutes. Store in a cool, dark place.

Spicy Carrot Chutney

- **P.T.:** 1 hour
- **Acidity level:** Moderate
- **Head Space:** 1/2 inch
- **Jar and Lid Preparation:** Sterilize jars and lids
- **Procedure:** Simmer grated carrots with apple cider vinegar, a touch of ginger, and a sugar substitute. Add red chili flakes for heat.
- **Ingr.:** 2 lb. carrots, grated; 1/4 Cups apple cider vinegar; 1 Tblsp ginger, minced; 1/4 Cups sugar substitute; 1 tsp red chili flakes.
- **Handling and Storage Instructions:** Process in a water bath for 15 minutes. Store in a cool, dark place.

Mixed Berry Jam

- **P.T.:** 1 hour
- **Acidity level:** Moderate
- **Head Space:** 1/4 inch
- **Jar and Lid Preparation:** Sterilize jars and lids
- **Procedure:** Cook a mix of berries with a sugar substitute and lemon juice. Stir in pectin until it reaches a jam consistency.
- **Ingr.:** 4 Cups mixed berries; 1/4 Cups lemon juice; 1 Cup sugar substitute; 1 package pectin.
- **Handling and Storage Instructions:** Process in a water bath for 10 minutes. Store in a cool, dark place.

Savory Eggplant Relish

- **P.T.:** 1 hour
- **Acidity level:** High
- **Head Space:** 1/2 inch
- **Jar and Lid Preparation:** Sterilize jars and lids
- **Procedure:** Roast eggplants and blend with tomatoes, garlic, and vinegar. Season with herbs and simmer until thick.
- **Ingr.:** 2 large eggplants, roasted; 2 tomatoes, chopped; 2 cloves garlic, minced; 1/4 Cups vinegar; 1 Tblsp herbs, minced.
- **Handling and Storage Instructions:** Process in a water bath for 15 minutes. Store in a cool, dark place.

Pear and Ginger Preserve

- **P.T.:** 1.5 hours
- **Acidity level:** Moderate
- **Head Space:** 1/4 inch
- **Jar and Lid Preparation:** Sterilize jars and lids
- **Procedure:** Combine diced pears with fresh ginger, lemon juice, and a sugar substitute. Cook until the pears soften and the mixture thickens.
- **Ingr.:** 4 lb. pears, peeled and diced; 2 Tblsp ginger, minced; 1/4 Cups lemon juice; 1/4 Cups sugar substitute.
- **Handling and Storage Instructions:** Process in a water bath for 10 minutes. Store in a cool, dark place.

Sweet Pepper Jelly

- **P.T.:** 50 minutes
- **Acidity level:** High
- **Head Space:** 1/4 inch

- **Jar and Lid Preparation:** Sterilize jars and lids
- **Procedure:** Simmer chopped sweet peppers with apple cider vinegar and a sugar substitute. Add pectin and cook until it gels.
- **Ingr.:** 2 Cups sweet peppers, chopped; 1/4 Cups apple cider vinegar; 1/4 Cups sugar substitute; 1 package pectin.
- **Handling and Storage Instructions:** Process in a water bath for 10 minutes. Store in a cool, dark place.

International Preserves: Exploring Global Canning Recipes

Moroccan Preserved Lemons

- **P.T.:** 30 minutes
- **Acidity level:** High
- **Head Space:** 1/4 inch
- **Jar and Lid Preparation:** Sterilize jars and lids
- **Procedure:** Quarter lemons almost to the base, stuff with sea salt. Pack tightly in jars, covering with lemon juice. Seal and leave to mature.

- **Ingr.:** 5 lemons; 1/4 Cups sea salt; Extra lemon juice for covering.
- **Handling and Storage Instructions:** Mature for at least 4 weeks. Refrigerate after opening.

Indian Mango Chutney

- **P.T.:** 1 hour
- **Acidity level:** Moderate
- **Head Space:** 1/2 inch
- **Jar and Lid Preparation:** Sterilize jars and lids
- **Procedure:** Combine diced mangoes, vinegar, sugar, ginger, garlic, and spices. Simmer until thickened.

- **Ingr.:** 3 ripe mangoes; 1 Cup vinegar; 1 Cup sugar; 2 Tblsp ginger, minced; 2 cloves garlic, minced; 1 tsp cinnamon; 1 tsp cloves; 1 tsp cumin.
- **Handling and Storage Instructions:** Process in a water bath for 15 minutes. Store in a cool, dark place.

Japanese Umeboshi (Pickled Plums)

- **P.T.:** Several days for drying
- **Acidity level:** High
- **Head Space:** 1/2 inch
- **Jar and Lid Preparation:** Sterilize jars and lids
- **Procedure:** Soak plums in brine, then dry under the sun. Pack in jars with pickling salt and shiso leaves.
- **Ingr.:** 2 lb. plums; 1/4 Cups pickling salt; Shiso leaves.
- **Handling and Storage Instructions:** Store in a cool, dark place. Mature for several months.

Italian Marinated Artichokes

- **P.T.:** 45 minutes
- **Acidity level:** Moderate
- **Head Space:** 1/2 inch
- **Jar and Lid Preparation:** Sterilize jars and lids
- **Procedure:** Blanch artichoke hearts in lemon water. Marinate in a mixture of olive oil, vinegar, herbs, and garlic. Pack into jars.
- **Ingr.:** 12 artichoke hearts; 2 lemons, juice; 1/2 Cups olive oil; 1/4 Cups vinegar; 1 Tblsp mixed herbs (oregano, thyme); 2 cloves garlic, minced.
- **Handling and Storage Instructions:** Process in a water bath for 10 minutes. Store in a cool, dark place.

French Ratatouille Preserve

- **P.T.:** 1.5 hours
- **Acidity level:** Low
- **Head Space:** 1 inch
- **Jar and Lid Preparation:** Sterilize jars and lids
- **Procedure:** Sauté eggplant, zucchini, bell peppers, onions, and tomatoes. Season with herbs and olive oil. Simmer until tender.

- **Ingr.:** 1 eggplant; 2 zucchinis; 1 red bell pepper; 1 yellow bell pepper; 2 onions; 4 tomatoes; 1/4 Cups olive oil; 1 Tblsp mixed herbs (basil, rosemary, thyme).
- **Handling and Storage Instructions:** Process in a pressure canner for 85 minutes. Store in a cool, dark place.

Mexican Salsa Verde

- **P.T.:** 40 minutes
- **Acidity level:** High
- **Head Space:** 1/2 inch
- **Jar and Lid Preparation:** Sterilize jars and lids
- **Procedure:** Roast tomatillos and jalapeños. Blend with lime juice, cilantro, and onions. Simmer and pack into jars.

- **Ingr.:** 1 lb. tomatillos; 2 jalapeños; 1/4 Cups lime juice; 1/2 Cups cilantro; 1 onion.
- **Handling and Storage Instructions:** Process in a water bath for 15 minutes. Store in a cool, dark place.

British Bramble Jelly

- **P.T.:** 1 hour
- **Acidity level:** Moderate
- **Head Space:** 1/4 inch
- **Jar and Lid Preparation:** Sterilize jars and lids
- **Procedure:** Cook blackberries with water until soft. Strain through a jelly bag. Add sugar and lemon juice, boil until it sets.
- **Ingr.:** 2 lb. blackberries; 1 Cup water; 2 Cups sugar; 1 lemon, juice.
- **Handling and Storage Instructions:** Process in a water bath for 10 minutes. Store in a cool, dark place.

Greek Olive Tapenade

- **P.T.:** 30 minutes
- **Acidity level:** Low
- **Head Space:** 1/2 inch
- **Jar and Lid Preparation:** Sterilize jars and lids
- **Procedure:** Blend pitted olives with capers, garlic, lemon juice, and olive oil. Season with herbs.
- **Ingr.:** 2 Cups pitted olives; 1 Tblsp capers; 2 cloves garlic; 2 Tblsp lemon juice; 1/2 Cups olive oil; 1 Tblsp mixed herbs (oregano, thyme).
- **Handling and Storage Instructions:** Process in a pressure canner for 75 minutes. Store in a cool, dark place.

Korean Kimchi

- **P.T.:** 2 days (for fermentation)
- **Acidity level:** High
- **Head Space:** 1 inch
- **Jar and Lid Preparation:** Sterilize jars and lids
- **Procedure:** Ferment Napa cabbage with Korean chili flakes, garlic, ginger, and fish sauce. Pack into jars and let ferment.
- **Ingr.:** 1 Napa cabbage; 1/4 Cups Korean chili flakes; 4 cloves garlic, minced; 2 Tblsp ginger, minced; 2 Tblsp fish sauce.
- **Handling and Storage Instructions:** Ferment at room temperature for 2 days, then refrigerate.

South African Chakalaka

- **P.T.:** 1 hour
- **Acidity level:** Moderate
- **Head Space:** 1/2 inch
- **Jar and Lid Preparation:** Sterilize jars and lids
- **Procedure:** Sauté onions, bell peppers, carrots, tomatoes, and spices. Cook until vegetables are tender.
- **Ingr.:** 2 onions; 2 bell peppers; 2 carrots; 4 tomatoes; 1 Tblsp curry powder.
- **Handling and Storage Instructions:** Process in a water bath for 15 minutes. Store in a cool, dark place.

Spanish Escabeche of Mackerel

- **P.T.:** 1 hour
- **Acidity level:** High
- **Head Space:** 1/2 inch
- **Jar and Lid Preparation:** Sterilize jars and lids
- **Procedure:** Marinate mackerel in a mixture of vinegar, olive oil, garlic, and bay leaves. Simmer gently, then pack into jars.

- **Ingr.:** 4 mackerel fillets; 1/2 Cups vinegar; 1/4 Cups olive oil; 2 cloves garlic; 2 bay leaves.
- **Handling and Storage Instructions:** Process in a water bath for 15 minutes. Store in a cool, dark place.

Thai Sweet Chili Sauce

- **P.T.:** 40 minutes
- **Acidity level:** Moderate
- **Head Space:** 1/2 inch
- **Jar and Lid Preparation:** Sterilize jars and lids
- **Procedure:** Blend fresh chili peppers with garlic, sugar, and vinegar. Boil until the mixture thickens.

- **Ingr.:** 10 chili peppers; 4 cloves garlic; 1 Cup sugar; 1/2 Cups vinegar.
- **Handling and Storage Instructions:** Process in a water bath for 10 minutes. Store in a cool, dark place.

Chinese Plum Sauce

- **P.T.:** 1.5 hours
- **Acidity level:** Moderate
- **Head Space:** 1/2 inch
- **Jar and Lid Preparation:** Sterilize jars and lids
- **Procedure:** Simmer plums with soy sauce, ginger, garlic, and spices. Blend until smooth, then cook until thickened.
- **Ingr.:** 2 lb. plums; 1/4 Cups soy sauce; 2 Tblsp ginger, minced; 2 cloves garlic, minced; 1 tsp five-spice powder.
- **Handling and Storage Instructions:** Process in a water bath for 15 minutes. Store in a cool, dark place.

Turkish Eggplant Pickle

- **P.T.:** 1 hour
- **Acidity level:** High
- **Head Space:** 1 inch
- **Jar and Lid Preparation:** Sterilize jars and lids
- **Procedure:** Roast eggplants, then pickle in a mixture of vinegar, garlic, and herbs. Pack into jars.
- **Ingr.:** 3 large eggplants; 1 Cup vinegar; 2 cloves garlic, minced; 1 Tblsp mixed herbs (parsley, dill).
- **Handling and Storage Instructions:** Process in a water bath for 10 minutes. Store in a cool, dark place.

German Sauerkraut

- **P.T.:** Several weeks (for fermentation)
- **Acidity level:** High
- **Head Space:** 1 inch
- **Jar and Lid Preparation:** Sterilize jars and lids
- **Procedure:** Ferment shredded cabbage with salt in a crock until sour. Pack into jars.
- **Ingr.:** 2 lb. cabbage; 2 Tblsp salt.
- **Handling and Storage Instructions:** Ferment at room temperature for several weeks, then refrigerate.

Brazilian Pepper Sauce

- **P.T.:** 30 minutes
- **Acidity level:** High
- **Head Space:** 1/2 inch
- **Jar and Lid Preparation:** Sterilize jars and lids
- **Procedure:** Blend Malagueta peppers with vinegar, garlic, and a pinch of salt. Boil briefly, then bottle.
- **Ingr.:** 1/2 Cups Malagueta peppers; 1 Cup vinegar; 2 cloves garlic; 1 tsp salt.
- **Handling and Storage Instructions:** Process in a water bath for 10 minutes. Store in a cool, dark place.

Russian Dill Pickles

- **P.T.:** 45 minutes
- **Acidity level:** High
- **Head Space:** 1/2 inch
- **Jar and Lid Preparation:** Sterilize jars and lids
- **Procedure:** Pack cucumbers, dill, garlic, and peppercorns in jars. Cover with a brine of vinegar, water, and salt. Seal and process.
- **Ingr.:** 2 lb. cucumbers; 1/4 Cups dill, minced; 4 cloves garlic, minced; 1 Tblsp peppercorns; 2 Cups vinegar; 2 Cups water; 1 Tblsp salt.
- **Handling and Storage Instructions:** Process in a water bath for 10 minutes. Store in a cool, dark place.

Filipino Atchara (Pickled Papaya)

- **P.T.:** 1 hour
- **Acidity level:** High
- **Head Space:** 1/2 inch
- **Jar and Lid Preparation:** Sterilize jars and lids
- **Procedure:** Shred green papaya and mix with carrots, bell peppers, and raisins. Pickle in a mixture of vinegar, sugar, and spices.
- **Ingr.:** 1 large green papaya; 2 carrots; 1 bell pepper; 1/2 Cups raisins; 1 Cup vinegar; 1/2 Cups sugar; 1 tsp salt; 1 Tblsp whole peppercorns.
- **Handling and Storage Instructions:** Process in a water bath for 15 minutes. Store in a cool, dark place.

Middle Eastern Fig Jam

- **P.T.:** 1 hour
- **Acidity level:** Moderate
- **Head Space:** 1/4 inch
- **Jar and Lid Preparation:** Sterilize jars and lids
- **Procedure:** Cook figs with lemon juice, honey, and spices until thick. Mash or blend to desired consistency.

- **Ingr.:** 2 lb. figs; 1/4 Cups lemon juice; 1 Cup honey; 1 tsp cinnamon.
- **Handling and Storage Instructions:** Process in a water bath for 10 minutes. Store in a cool, dark place.

Hungarian Pepper and Tomato Relish (Lecsó)

- **P.T.:** 1 hour
- **Acidity level:** Moderate
- **Head Space:** 1/2 inch
- **Jar and Lid Preparation:** Sterilize jars and lids
- **Procedure:** Sauté bell peppers, tomatoes, and onions. Season with paprika and simmer until soft. Pack into jars.

- **Ingr.:** 2 bell peppers; 4 tomatoes; 1 onion; 2 Tblsp paprika.
- **Handling and Storage Instructions:** Process in a water bath for 15 minutes. Store in a cool, dark place.

Caribbean Pineapple Jam

- **P.T.:** 1 hour
- **Acidity level:** Moderate
- **Head Space:** 1/4 inch
- **Jar and Lid Preparation:** Sterilize jars and lids
- **Procedure:** Simmer chopped pineapple with lime juice and a hint of cinnamon. Add sugar and pectin, cooking until thickened.
- **Ingr.:** 1 large pineapple; 2 limes juice; 1 tsp cinnamon; 2 Cups sugar; 1 package pectin.
- **Handling and Storage Instructions:** Process in a water bath for 10 minutes. Store in a cool, dark place.

Swedish Lingonberry Preserve

- **P.T.:** 50 minutes
- **Acidity level:** Moderate
- **Head Space:** 1/4 inch
- **Jar and Lid Preparation:** Sterilize jars and lids
- **Procedure:** Cook lingonberries with water and sugar until berries burst and the sauce thickens.
- **Ingr.:** 2 Cups lingonberries; 1 Cup water; 1 Cup sugar.
- **Handling and Storage Instructions:** Process in a water bath for 10 minutes. Store in a cool, dark place.

Egyptian Lemon and Mint Jelly

- **P.T.:** 45 minutes
- **Acidity level:** High
- **Head Space:** 1/4 inch
- **Jar and Lid Preparation:** Sterilize jars and lids
- **Procedure:** Combine lemon juice, chopped mint, sugar, and pectin. Boil until it sets into a jelly.
- **Ingr.:** 1 Cup lemon juice; 1/4 Cups mint, chopped; 2 Cups sugar; 1 package pectin.
- **Handling and Storage Instructions:** Process in a water bath for 10 minutes. Store in a cool, dark place.

Peruvian Aji Amarillo Sauce

- **P.T.:** 40 minutes
- **Acidity level:** High
- **Head Space:** 1/2 inch
- **Jar and Lid Preparation:** Sterilize jars and lids
- **Procedure:** Blend Aji Amarillo peppers with vinegar, lime juice, and garlic. Simmer until slightly thickened.
- **Ingr.:** 1/2 Cups Aji Amarillo peppers; 1/4 Cups vinegar; 2 limes, juice; 2 cloves garlic.
- **Handling and Storage Instructions:** Process in a water bath for 10 minutes. Store in a cool, dark place.

Australian Lemon Myrtle Marmalade

- **P.T.:** 1 hour
- **Acidity level:** High
- **Head Space:** 1/4 inch
- **Jar and Lid Preparation:** Sterilize jars and lids
- **Procedure:** Cook lemon myrtle leaves with lemon zest and juice, adding sugar and water. Boil until it reaches a marmalade consistency.
- **Ingr.:** 1/4 Cups lemon myrtle leaves; 2 lemons, zest and juice; 2 Cups sugar; 1 Cup water.
- **Handling and Storage Instructions:** Process in a water bath for 10 minutes. Store in a cool, dark place.

Polish Dill Pickle Soup Concentrate

- **P.T.:** 1.5 hours
- **Acidity level:** Moderate
- **Head Space:** 1 inch
- **Jar and Lid Preparation:** Sterilize jars and lids
- **Procedure:** Simmer diced pickles, potatoes, carrots, and vegetable broth. Blend to a smooth concentrate for soup.
- **Ingr.:** 1 Cup diced pickles; 2 potatoes; 2 carrots; 4 Cups vegetable broth.
- **Handling and Storage Instructions:** Process in a pressure canner for 70 minutes. Store in a cool, dark place.

Indonesian Sambal Oelek

- **P.T.:** 30 minutes
- **Acidity level:** High
- **Head Space:** 1/2 inch
- **Jar and Lid Preparation:** Sterilize jars and lids
- **Procedure:** Grind fresh red chilies with a bit of vinegar and salt. Simmer until the mixture thickens.
- **Ingr.:** 2 Cups red chilies; 1/4 Cups vinegar; 1 tsp salt.
- **Handling and Storage Instructions:** Process in a water bath for 10 minutes. Store in a cool, dark place.

Korean Pear and Ginger Jam

- **P.T.:** 1 hour
- **Acidity level:** Moderate
- **Head Space:** 1/4 inch
- **Jar and Lid Preparation:** Sterilize jars and lids
- **Procedure:** Cook Korean pears with grated ginger, lemon juice, and sugar until thickened into a jam.
- **Ingr.:** 2 Korean pears; 2 Tblsp ginger, grated; 1 lemon, juice; 2 Cups sugar.
- **Handling and Storage Instructions:** Process in a water bath for 10 minutes. Store in a cool, dark place.

Bulgarian Rose Petal Jam

- **P.T.:** 1 hour
- **Acidity level:** Moderate
- **Head Space:** 1/4 inch
- **Jar and Lid Preparation:** Sterilize jars and lids
- **Procedure:** Simmer edible rose petals with sugar and lemon juice, adding a touch of water. Cook until it sets into a jam.

- **Ingr.:** 2 Cups edible rose petals; 1 Cup sugar; 2 lemons, juice; 1/2 Cups water.
- **Handling and Storage Instructions:** Process in a water bath for 10 minutes. Store in a cool, dark place.

Lebanese Pickled Turnips

- **P.T.:** 45 minutes
- **Acidity level:** High
- **Head Space:** 1/2 inch
- **Jar and Lid Preparation:** Sterilize jars and lids
- **Procedure:** Slice turnips and pack into jars with beet slices, garlic, and spices. Cover with a brine of vinegar, water, and salt.

- **Ingr.:** 4 turnips; 1 beet; 2 cloves garlic; 1 Cup vinegar; 1 Cup water; 2 Tblsp salt.
- **Handling and Storage Instructions:** Process in a water bath for 10 minutes. Store in a cool, dark place.

Sweet and Savory Spreads: Expanding Your Flavor Palette

Roasted Red Pepper Hummus

- **P.T.:** 45 minutes
- **Acidity level:** Low
- **Head Space:** 1/2 inch
- **Jar and Lid Preparation:** Sterilize jars and lids
- **Procedure:** Blend roasted red peppers with chickpeas, tahini, lemon juice, and garlic. Adjust seasoning and pack into jars.
- **Ingr.:** 4 roasted red peppers; 2 Cups cooked chickpeas; 1/2 Cups tahini; 1/4 Cups lemon juice; 2 cloves garlic, minced; Salt to taste.
- **Handling and Storage Instructions:** Process in a pressure canner for 75 minutes. Store in a cool, dark place.

Blackberry Lavender Butter

- **P.T.:** 1 hour
- **Acidity level:** Moderate
- **Head Space:** 1/4 inch
- **Jar and Lid Preparation:** Sterilize jars and lids
- **Procedure:** Simmer blackberries with sugar, a splash of lemon juice, and lavender buds until thickened. Strain and jar.
- **Ingr.:** 3 Cups blackberries; 1 Cup sugar; 2 Tblsp lemon juice; 1 Tblsp lavender buds.
- **Handling and Storage Instructions:** Process in a water bath for 10 minutes. Store in a cool, dark place.

Caramelized Onion and Fig Spread

- **P.T.:** 1.5 hours
- **Acidity level:** Low
- **Head Space:** 1/2 inch
- **Jar and Lid Preparation:** Sterilize jars and lids
- **Procedure:** Slowly caramelize onions, then add chopped figs, balsamic vinegar, and a hint of thyme. Cook until jammy.
- **Ingr.:** 3 large onions, thinly sliced; 1 Cup chopped figs; 1/4 Cups balsamic vinegar; 1 tsp fresh thyme.
- **Handling and Storage Instructions:** Process in a pressure canner for 85 minutes. Store in a cool, dark place.

Bourbon Peach Preserve

- **P.T.:** 1 hour
- **Acidity level:** Moderate
- **Head Space:** 1/4 inch
- **Jar and Lid Preparation:** Sterilize jars and lids
- **Procedure:** Simmer peaches with bourbon, lemon juice, and sugar until thickened. Mash to desired consistency.
- **Ingr.:** 4 Cups peaches, peeled and chopped; 1/2 Cups bourbon; 1/4 Cups lemon juice; 1 Cup sugar.
- **Handling and Storage Instructions:** Process in a water bath for 10 minutes. Store in a cool, dark place.

Creamy Herb Cheese Spread

- **P.T.:** 30 minutes
- **Acidity level:** Low
- **Head Space:** 1/2 inch
- **Jar and Lid Preparation:** Sterilize jars and lids
- **Procedure:** Blend soft cheese with a mix of fresh herbs, garlic, and a splash of lemon juice. Pack into jars.

- **Ingr.:** 2 Cups soft cheese; 1/4 Cups mixed fresh herbs (basil, chives, parsley); 1 clove garlic, minced; 1 Tblsp lemon juice.
- **Handling and Storage Instructions:** Process in a pressure canner for 60 minutes. Store in a cool, dark place.

Maple Pumpkin Butter

- **P.T.:** 1 hour
- **Acidity level:** Moderate
- **Head Space:** 1/4 inch
- **Jar and Lid Preparation:** Sterilize jars and lids
- **Procedure:** Cook pumpkin puree with maple syrup, spices, and a dash of lemon juice until thick. Stir frequently.

- **Ingr.:** 4 Cups pumpkin puree; 1/2 Cups maple syrup; 1 tsp cinnamon; 1/4 tsp nutmeg; 1 Tblsp lemon juice.
- **Handling and Storage Instructions:** Process in a water bath for 10 minutes. Store in a cool, dark place.

Jalapeño Apple Jelly

- **P.T.:** 1 hour
- **Acidity level:** High
- **Head Space:** 1/4 inch
- **Jar and Lid Preparation:** Sterilize jars and lids
- **Procedure:** Cook apple juice with chopped jalapeños, vinegar, and pectin. Boil until it sets into a jelly.

- **Ingr.:** 2 Cups apple juice; 1 Cup chopped jalapeños; 1/4 Cups vinegar; 1 package pectin.
- **Handling and Storage Instructions:** Process in a water bath for 10 minutes. Store in a cool, dark place.

Balsamic Fig and Olive Tapenade

- **P.T.:** 40 minutes
- **Acidity level:** Low
- **Head Space:** 1/2 inch
- **Jar and Lid Preparation:** Sterilize jars and lids
- **Procedure:** Blend chopped figs and olives with balsamic vinegar, capers, and a touch of honey. Achieve a chunky consistency.

- **Ingr.:** 1 Cup chopped figs; 1 Cup chopped olives; 1/4 Cups balsamic vinegar; 1 Tblsp capers 1 Tblsp honey.
- **Handling and Storage Instructions:** Process in a pressure canner for 75 minutes. Store in a cool, dark place.

Sun-Dried Tomato and Basil Pesto

- **P.T.:** 30 minutes
- **Acidity level:** Low
- **Head Space:** 1/2 inch
- **Jar and Lid Preparation:** Sterilize jars and lids
- **Procedure:** Blend sun-dried tomatoes, fresh basil, pine nuts, Parmesan cheese, and olive oil. Season with garlic and a pinch of salt.
- **Ingr.:** 1 Cup sun-dried tomatoes; 1 Cup fresh basil leaves; 1/4 Cups pine nuts; 1/4 Cups grated Parmesan cheese; 1/2 Cups olive oil; 2 cloves garlic; Salt to taste.
- **Handling and Storage Instructions:** Process in a pressure canner for 60 minutes. Store in a cool, dark place.

Apple and Cinnamon Butter

- **P.T.:** 1 hour
- **Acidity level:** Moderate
- **Head Space:** 1/4 inch
- **Jar and Lid Preparation:** Sterilize jars and lids
- **Procedure:** Cook down apples with cinnamon, sugar, and a splash of lemon juice until thick and spreadable.
- **Ingr.:** 4 Cups apples, peeled and chopped; 1 tsp cinnamon; 1 Cup sugar; 2 Tblsp lemon juice.
- **Handling and Storage Instructions:** Process in a water bath for 10 minutes. Store in a cool, dark place.

Raspberry and Rose Jam

- **P.T.:** 50 minutes
- **Acidity level:** Moderate
- **Head Space:** 1/4 inch
- **Jar and Lid Preparation:** Sterilize jars and lids
- **Procedure:** Simmer raspberries with rose water, sugar, and lemon juice. Add pectin and boil until set.
- **Ingr.:** 3 Cups raspberries; 1/4 Cups rose water; 2 Cups sugar; 1/4 Cups lemon juice; 1 package pectin.
- **Handling and Storage Instructions:** Process in a water bath for 10 minutes. Store in a cool, dark place.

Garlic and Herb Cheese Spread

- **P.T.:** 30 minutes
- **Acidity level:** Low
- **Head Space:** 1/2 inch
- **Jar and Lid Preparation:** Sterilize jars and lids
- **Procedure:** Blend soft cheese with a variety of fresh herbs, minced garlic, and a bit of lemon juice. Adjust seasoning.
- **Ingr.:** 2 Cups soft cheese; 1/4 Cups mixed fresh herbs (dill, parsley, chives); 2 cloves garlic, minced; 1 Tblsp lemon juice.
- **Handling and Storage Instructions:** Process in a pressure canner for 60 minutes. Store in a cool, dark place.

Pear and Vanilla Bean Jam

- **P.T.:** 1 hour
- **Acidity level:** Moderate
- **Head Space:** 1/4 inch
- **Jar and Lid Preparation:** Sterilize jars and lids
- **Procedure:** Cook chopped pears with scraped vanilla bean pods, sugar, and lemon juice. Mash to desired consistency.

- **Ingr.:** 4 Cups pears, peeled and chopped; 2 vanilla beans, split and scraped; 1 Cup sugar; 1/4 Cups lemon juice.
- **Handling and Storage Instructions:** Process in a water bath for 10 minutes. Store in a cool, dark place.

Spiced Carrot Spread

- **P.T.:** 1 hour
- **Acidity level:** Moderate
- **Head Space:** 1/2 inch
- **Jar and Lid Preparation:** Sterilize jars and lids
- **Procedure:** Simmer grated carrots with orange juice, sugar, cinnamon, and nutmeg until thickened. Blend to a smooth consistency.

- **Ingr.:** 3 Cups carrots, grated; 1/2 Cups orange juice; 1 Cup sugar; 1 tsp cinnamon; 1/2 tsp nutmeg.
- **Handling and Storage Instructions:** Process in a water bath for 15 minutes. Store in a cool, dark place.

Blueberry Lavender Butter

- **P.T.:** 1 hour
- **Acidity level:** Moderate
- **Head Space:** 1/4 inch
- **Jar and Lid Preparation:** Sterilize jars and lids
- **Procedure:** Cook blueberries with sugar, lemon juice, and culinary lavender until thick. Strain for a smooth texture.
- **Ingr.:** 3 Cups blueberries; 1 Cup sugar; 2 Tblsp lemon juice; 1 Tblsp culinary lavender.
- **Handling and Storage Instructions:** Process in a water bath for 10 minutes. Store in a cool, dark place.

Mint and Pea Pesto

- **P.T.:** 30 minutes
- **Acidity level:** Low
- **Head Space:** 1/2 inch
- **Jar and Lid Preparation:** Sterilize jars and lids
- **Procedure:** Blend cooked peas with fresh mint, Parmesan cheese, garlic, and olive oil. Season with lemon juice and salt.
- **Ingr.:** 2 Cups cooked peas; 1/4 Cups fresh mint leaves; 1/4 Cups grated Parmesan cheese; 1 clove garlic, minced; 1/2 Cups olive oil; 2 Tblsp lemon juice; Salt to taste
- **Handling and Storage Instructions:** Process in a pressure canner for 60 minutes. Store in a cool, dark place.

Cherry and Almond Conserve

- **P.T.:** 1 hour
- **Acidity level:** Moderate
- **Head Space:** 1/4 inch
- **Jar and Lid Preparation:** Sterilize jars and lids
- **Procedure:** Simmer pitted cherries with sugar, lemon juice, and chopped almonds. Cook until the mixture thickens.
- **Ingr.:** 3 Cups pitted cherries; 1 Cup sugar; 1/4 Cups lemon juice; 1/2 Cups chopped almonds.
- **Handling and Storage Instructions:** Process in a water bath for 10 minutes. Store in a cool, dark place.

Smoky Eggplant Spread

- **P.T.:** 1 hour
- **Acidity level:** Low
- **Head Space:** 1/2 inch
- **Jar and Lid Preparation:** Sterilize jars and lids
- **Procedure:** Roast eggplants until tender. Blend with tahini, garlic, lemon juice, and a hint of smoked paprika.
- **Ingr.:** 3 large eggplants, roasted; 1/4 Cups tahini; 2 cloves garlic, minced; 1/4 Cups lemon juice; 1 tsp smoked paprika.
- **Handling and Storage Instructions:** Process in a pressure canner for 70 minutes. Store in a cool, dark place.

Spicy Mango Chutney

- **P.T.:** 1 hour
- **Acidity level:** High
- **Head Space:** 1/2 inch
- **Jar and Lid Preparation:** Sterilize jars and lids
- **Procedure:** Simmer diced mangoes with sugar, vinegar, ginger, garlic, and chili flakes. Cook until thick and jam-like.
- **Ingr.:** 3 Cups mangoes, peeled and diced; 1 Cup sugar; 1/2 Cups vinegar; 1 Tblsp ginger, minced; 2 cloves garlic, minced; 1 tsp chili flakes.
- **Handling and Storage Instructions:** Process in a water bath for 15 minutes. Store in a cool, dark place.

Fig and Port Wine Jam

- **P.T.:** 1 hour
- **Acidity level:** Moderate
- **Head Space:** 1/4 inch
- **Jar and Lid Preparation:** Sterilize jars and lids
- **Procedure:** Cook down figs with port wine, sugar, and a squeeze of lemon juice. Mash to desired consistency.
- **Ingr.:** 3 Cups figs, chopped; 1/2 Cups port wine; 1 Cup sugar; 1 Tblsp lemon juice.
- **Handling and Storage Instructions:** Process in a water bath for 10 minutes. Store in a cool, dark place.

Roasted Garlic Aioli

- **P.T.:** 40 minutes
- **Acidity level:** Low
- **Head Space:** 1/2 inch
- **Jar and Lid Preparation:** Sterilize jars and lids
- **Procedure:** Blend roasted garlic with egg yolks, olive oil, lemon juice, and a pinch of salt. Achieve a creamy texture.
- **Ingr.:** 1 head garlic, roasted; 2 egg yolks; 1 Cup olive oil; 2 Tblsp lemon juice; Salt to taste.
- **Handling and Storage Instructions:** Process in a pressure canner for 60 minutes. Store in a cool, dark place.

Cranberry Orange Relish

- **P.T.:** 45 minutes
- **Acidity level:** High
- **Head Space:** 1/2 inch
- **Jar and Lid Preparation:** Sterilize jars and lids
- **Procedure:** Cook cranberries with orange zest and juice, sugar, and water until berries pop and mixture thickens.
- **Ingr.:** 2 Cups cranberries; 1 orange, zest and juice; 1 Cup sugar; 1/2 Cups water.
- **Handling and Storage Instructions:** Process in a water bath for 15 minutes. Store in a cool, dark place.

Beetroot and Horseradish Spread

- **P.T.:** 1 hour
- **Acidity level:** Low
- **Head Space:** 1/2 inch
- **Jar and Lid Preparation:** Sterilize jars and lids
- **Procedure:** Blend roasted beetroots with grated horseradish, vinegar, and a touch of sugar. Adjust consistency.
- **Ingr.:** 3 Cups beetroots, roasted and peeled; 1/4 Cups grated horseradish; 1/4 Cups vinegar; 1 Tblsp sugar.
- **Handling and Storage Instructions:** Process in a pressure canner for 70 minutes. Store in a cool, dark place.

Green Tomato and Apple Chutney

- **P.T.:** 1.5 hours
- **Acidity level:** Moderate
- **Head Space:** 1/2 inch
- **Jar and Lid Preparation:** Sterilize jars and lids
- **Procedure:** Simmer chopped green tomatoes and apples with onions, raisins, vinegar, sugar, and spices until thick.
- **Ingr.:** 2 Cups green tomatoes, chopped; 2 Cups apples, chopped; 1 onion, diced; 1/2 Cups raisins; 1 Cup vinegar; 1 Cup sugar; 1 tsp cinnamon; 1 tsp ginger.
- **Handling and Storage Instructions:** Process in a water bath for 15 minutes. Store in a cool, dark place.

Zucchini and Lemon Marmalade

- **P.T.:** 1 hour
- **Acidity level:** High
- **Head Space:** 1/4 inch
- **Jar and Lid Preparation:** Sterilize jars and lids
- **Procedure:** Cook grated zucchini with lemon zest and juice, sugar, and water until it reaches a marmalade consistency.
- **Ingr.:** 4 Cups zucchini, grated; 2 lemons, zest and juice; 2 Cups sugar; 1/2 Cups water.
- **Handling and Storage Instructions:** Process in a water bath for 10 minutes. Store in a cool, dark place.

Pumpkin Spice Spread

- **P.T.:** 1 hour
- **Acidity level:** Moderate
- **Head Space:** 1/4 inch
- **Jar and Lid Preparation:** Sterilize jars and lids
- **Procedure:** Simmer pumpkin puree with sugar, a blend of pumpkin pie spices, and a dash of lemon juice until thickened.
- **Ingr.:** 4 Cups pumpkin puree; 2 Cups sugar; 1 Tblsp pumpkin pie spice; 1 Tblsp lemon juice.
- **Handling and Storage Instructions:** Process in a water bath for 10 minutes. Store in a cool, dark place.

Black Olive Tapenade

- **P.T.:** 30 minutes
- **Acidity level:** Low
- **Head Space:** 1/2 inch
- **Jar and Lid Preparation:** Sterilize jars and lids
- **Procedure:** Blend pitted black olives with capers, anchovies, garlic, and olive oil. Season with lemon juice and herbs.
- **Ingr.:** 2 Cups black olives, pitted; 1/4 Cups capers; 4 anchovy fillets; 2 cloves garlic, minced; 1/2 Cups olive oil; 2 Tblsp lemon juice; 1 Tblsp mixed herbs (parsley, thyme).
- **Handling and Storage Instructions:** Process in a pressure canner for 60 minutes. Store in a cool, dark place.

Pear and Saffron Chutney

- **P.T.:** 1 hour
- **Acidity level:** Moderate
- **Head Space:** 1/2 inch
- **Jar and Lid Preparation:** Sterilize jars and lids
- **Procedure:** Cook diced pears with saffron threads, vinegar, sugar, and ginger. Simmer until thick and aromatic.
- **Ingr.:** 4 large pears, diced; 1 pinch saffron threads; 1 Cup vinegar; 1 Cup sugar; 1 Tblsp ginger, minced.
- **Handling and Storage Instructions:** Process in a water bath for 15 minutes. Store in a cool, dark place.

Caramel Apple Butter

- **P.T.:** 1.5 hours
- **Acidity level:** Moderate
- **Head Space:** 1/4 inch
- **Jar and Lid Preparation:** Sterilize jars and lids
- **Procedure:** Slow-cook apples with caramel sauce, cinnamon, and a splash of vanilla extract. Puree until smooth.
- **Ingr.:** 5 lb. apples, peeled and chopped; 1 Cup caramel sauce; 1 tsp cinnamon; 1 tsp vanilla extract.
- **Handling and Storage Instructions:** Process in a water bath for 10 minutes. Store in a cool, dark place.

Savory Bacon Jam

- **P.T.:** 1 hour
- **Acidity level:** Low
- **Head Space:** 1/2 inch
- **Jar and Lid Preparation:** Sterilize jars and lids
- **Procedure:** Cook chopped bacon with onions, brown sugar, coffee, and vinegar. Simmer until it forms a thick jam.
- **Ingr.:** 1 lb. bacon, chopped; 2 large onions, diced; 1 Cup brown sugar; 1/2 Cups coffee; 1/2 Cups vinegar.
- **Handling and Storage Instructions:** Process in a pressure canner for 75 minutes. Store in a cool, dark place.

Preserving Herbs and Spices: Oils, Vinegars, and Infusions

Rosemary Infused Olive Oil

- **P.T.:** 30 minutes
- **Acidity level:** Low
- **Head Space:** 1/2 inch
- **Jar and Lid Preparation:** Sterilize jars and lids
- **Procedure:** Gently warm olive oil with fresh rosemary sprigs. Let simmer lightly, then cool and strain into jars.
- **Ingr.:** 2 Cups olive oil; 4 sprigs fresh rosemary.
- **Handling and Storage Instructions:** Store in a cool, dark place. Use within 1 month.

Lemon and Thyme Vinegar

- **P.T.:** 40 minutes
- **Acidity level:** High
- **Head Space:** 1/2 inch
- **Jar and Lid Preparation:** Sterilize jars and lids
- **Procedure:** Infuse white wine vinegar with lemon zest and fresh thyme. Let sit for a few weeks, then strain and bottle.
- **Ingr.:** 2 Cups white wine vinegar; Zest of 2 lemons; 4 sprigs fresh thyme.
- **Handling and Storage Instructions:** Store in a cool, dark place. Best used within 6 months.

Spicy Garlic Chili Oil

- **P.T.:** 30 minutes
- **Acidity level:** Low
- **Head Space:** 1/2 inch
- **Jar and Lid Preparation:** Sterilize jars and lids
- **Procedure:** Heat olive oil with dried chili flakes and minced garlic. Cool, strain, and pour into jars.

- **Ingr.:** 2 Cups olive oil; 2 Tblsp dried chili flakes; 4 cloves garlic, minced.
- **Handling and Storage Instructions:** Store in a cool, dark place. Use within 1 month.

Basil and Pine Nut Pesto Oil

- **P.T.:** 30 minutes
- **Acidity level:** Low
- **Head Space:** 1/2 inch
- **Jar and Lid Preparation:** Sterilize jars and lids
- **Procedure:** Blend fresh basil, toasted pine nuts, Parmesan cheese, and olive oil. Season with salt and lemon juice.

- **Ingr.:** 2 Cups fresh basil leaves; 1/2 Cups toasted pine nuts; 1/2 Cups grated Parmesan cheese; 1 Cup olive oil; 1 tsp salt; 2 Tblsp lemon juice.
- **Handling and Storage Instructions:** Store in a cool, dark place. Use within 2 weeks.

Herb Infused Vinegar Mix

- **P.T.:** 45 minutes
- **Acidity level:** High
- **Head Space:** 1/2 inch
- **Jar and Lid Preparation:** Sterilize jars and lids
- **Procedure:** Combine a mix of fresh herbs (like dill, parsley, and tarragon) in apple cider vinegar. Let infuse, then strain.
- **Ingr.:** 2 Cups apple cider vinegar; 1/4 Cups chopped fresh dill; 1/4 Cups chopped fresh parsley; 1/4 Cups chopped fresh tarragon.
- **Handling and Storage Instructions:** Store in a cool, dark place. Best used within 6 months.

Citrus Zest Olive Oil

- **P.T.:** 30 minutes
- **Acidity level:** Low
- **Head Space:** 1/2 inch
- **Jar and Lid Preparation:** Sterilize jars and lids
- **Procedure:** Infuse olive oil with a mix of citrus zests (orange, lemon, lime). Gently heat, cool, and strain into jars.
- **Ingr.:** 2 Cups olive oil; Zest of 1 orange; Zest of 1 lemon; Zest of 1 lime.
- **Handling and Storage Instructions:** Store in a cool, dark place. Use within 1 month.

Vanilla Bean and Cinnamon Oil

- **P.T.:** 30 minutes
- **Acidity level:** Low
- **Head Space:** 1/2 inch
- **Jar and Lid Preparation:** Sterilize jars and lids
- **Procedure:** Warm olive oil with vanilla bean pods and cinnamon sticks. Let infuse, cool, and strain into jars.
- **Ingr.:** 2 Cups olive oil; 2 vanilla bean pods, split; 2 cinnamon sticks.
- **Handling and Storage Instructions:** Store in a cool, dark place. Use within 1 month.

Hot Pepper Vinegar

- **P.T.:** 35 minutes
- **Acidity level:** High
- **Head Space:** 1/2 inch
- **Jar and Lid Preparation:** Sterilize jars and lids
- **Procedure:** Pack jars with sliced hot peppers. Pour over heated white vinegar. Seal and let infuse.
- **Ingr.:** 2 Cups white vinegar; 4 sliced hot peppers.
- **Handling and Storage Instructions:** Store in a cool, dark place. Best used within 6 months.

Mint and Lemon Balm Tincture

- **P.T.:** 20 minutes
- **Acidity level:** Low
- **Head Space:** 1/2 inch
- **Jar and Lid Preparation:** Sterilize jars and lids
- **Procedure:** Soak fresh mint and lemon balm leaves in high-proof alcohol. Seal and let sit for several weeks. Strain and bottle.
- **Ingr.:** 1 Cup high-proof alcohol; 1/2 Cups fresh mint leaves; 1/2 Cups fresh lemon balm leaves.
- **Handling and Storage Instructions:** Store in a cool, dark place. Use as needed.

Savory Sage and Rosemary Oil

- **P.T.:** 30 minutes
- **Acidity level:** Low
- **Head Space:** 1/2 inch
- **Jar and Lid Preparation:** Sterilize jars and lids
- **Procedure:** Gently heat olive oil with fresh sage leaves and rosemary sprigs. Cool, strain, and pour into jars.
- **Ingr.:** 2 Cups olive oil; 4 sprigs fresh sage; 4 sprigs fresh rosemary.
- **Handling and Storage Instructions:** Store in a cool, dark place. Use within 1 month.

Chive Blossom Vinegar

- **P.T.:** 40 minutes
- **Acidity level:** High
- **Head Space:** 1/2 inch
- **Jar and Lid Preparation:** Sterilize jars and lids
- **Procedure:** Steep chive blossoms in white wine vinegar for a few weeks. Strain and bottle the infused vinegar.

- **Ingr.:** 2 Cups white wine vinegar; 1 Cup chive blossoms.
- **Handling and Storage Instructions:** Store in a cool, dark place. Best used within 1 year.

Oregano and Garlic Olive Oil

- **P.T.:** 30 minutes
- **Acidity level:** Low
- **Head Space:** 1/2 inch
- **Jar and Lid Preparation:** Sterilize jars and lids
- **Procedure:** Gently warm olive oil with fresh oregano and minced garlic. Cool, strain, and pour into jars.

- **Ingr.:** 2 Cups olive oil; 1/4 Cups fresh oregano leaves; 4 cloves garlic, minced.
- **Handling and Storage Instructions:** Store in a cool, dark place. Use within 1 month.

Ginger and Turmeric Infusion

- **P.T.:** 45 minutes
- **Acidity level:** Low
- **Head Space:** 1/2 inch
- **Jar and Lid Preparation:** Sterilize jars and lids
- **Procedure:** Simmer slices of fresh ginger and turmeric in a neutral oil. Cool, strain, and bottle.
- **Ingr.:** 2 Cups neutral oil (like grapeseed); 1/4 Cups fresh ginger, sliced; 1/4 Cups fresh turmeric, sliced.
- **Handling and Storage Instructions:** Store in a cool, dark place. Use within 2 months.

Cilantro Lime Vinegar

- **P.T.:** 35 minutes
- **Acidity level:** High
- **Head Space:** 1/2 inch
- **Jar and Lid Preparation:** Sterilize jars and lids
- **Procedure:** Infuse apple cider vinegar with fresh cilantro and lime zest. Let sit for several weeks, then strain and bottle.
- **Ingr.:** 2 Cups apple cider vinegar; 1/2 Cups fresh cilantro; Zest of 2 limes.
- **Handling and Storage Instructions:** Store in a cool, dark place. Best used within 6 months.

Fennel Seed and Orange Oil

- **P.T.:** 30 minutes
- **Acidity level:** Low
- **Head Space:** 1/2 inch
- **Jar and Lid Preparation:** Sterilize jars and lids
- **Procedure:** Gently heat olive oil with toasted fennel seeds and orange zest. Cool, strain, and pour into jars.

- **Ingr.:** 2 Cups olive oil; 2 Tblsp toasted fennel seeds; Zest of 1 orange.
- **Handling and Storage Instructions:** Store in a cool, dark place. Use within 1 month.

Rose and Peppercorn Vinegar

- **P.T.:** 40 minutes
- **Acidity level:** High
- **Head Space:** 1/2 inch
- **Jar and Lid Preparation:** Sterilize jars and lids
- **Procedure:** Steep dried rose petals and pink peppercorns in white vinegar. Let infuse, then strain and bottle.

- **Ingr.:** 2 Cups white vinegar; 1/4 Cups dried rose petals; 2 Tblsp pink peppercorns.
- **Handling and Storage Instructions:** Store in a cool, dark place. Best used within 1 year.

Lemongrass and Ginger Oil

- **P.T.:** 30 minutes
- **Acidity level:** Low
- **Head Space:** 1/2 inch
- **Jar and Lid Preparation:** Sterilize jars and lids
- **Procedure:** Simmer chopped lemongrass and ginger in a neutral oil. Strain and bottle the fragrant oil.
- **Ingr.:** 2 Cups neutral oil; 1/4 Cups fresh lemongrass, chopped; 1/4 Cups fresh ginger, grated.
- **Handling and Storage Instructions:** Store in a cool, dark place. Use within 2 months.

Tarragon and Mustard Seed Vinegar

- **P.T.:** 45 minutes
- **Acidity level:** High
- **Head Space:** 1/2 inch
- **Jar and Lid Preparation:** Sterilize jars and lids
- **Procedure:** Infuse white wine vinegar with fresh tarragon leaves and mustard seeds. Let sit for a few weeks, then strain and bottle.
- **Ingr.:** 2 Cups white wine vinegar; 1/4 Cups fresh tarragon leaves; 2 Tblsp mustard seeds.
- **Handling and Storage Instructions:** Store in a cool, dark place. Best used within 6 months.

Basil and Lemon Balm Vinegar

- **P.T.:** 40 minutes
- **Acidity level:** High
- **Head Space:** 1/2 inch
- **Jar and Lid Preparation:** Sterilize jars and lids
- **Procedure:** Steep fresh basil and lemon balm in apple cider vinegar. After several weeks, strain and bottle.

- **Ingr.:** 2 Cups apple cider vinegar; 1/2 Cups fresh basil leaves; 1/2 Cups fresh lemon balm leaves.
- **Handling and Storage Instructions:** Store in a cool, dark place. Best used within 1 year.

Spiced Apple Cider Vinegar

- **P.T.:** 50 minutes
- **Acidity level:** High
- **Head Space:** 1/2 inch
- **Jar and Lid Preparation:** Sterilize jars and lids
- **Procedure:** Combine apple cider vinegar with cinnamon sticks, star anise, and cloves. Heat gently, then let cool and strain.

- **Ingr.:** 2 Cups apple cider vinegar; 2 cinnamon sticks; 4 star anise; 4 cloves.
- **Handling and Storage Instructions:** Store in a cool, dark place. Best used within 1 year.

Dill and Lemon Infused Oil

- **P.T.:** 30 minutes
- **Acidity level:** Low
- **Head Space:** 1/2 inch
- **Jar and Lid Preparation:** Sterilize jars and lids
- **Procedure:** Warm olive oil with fresh dill and lemon zest. Allow to infuse, cool, then strain into jars.
- **Ingr.:** 2 Cups olive oil; 1/4 Cups fresh dill; Zest of 1 lemon.
- **Handling and Storage Instructions:** Store in a cool, dark place. Use within 1 month.

Coriander Seed Vinegar

- **P.T.:** 40 minutes
- **Acidity level:** High
- **Head Space:** 1/2 inch
- **Jar and Lid Preparation:** Sterilize jars and lids
- **Procedure:** Infuse white wine vinegar with toasted coriander seeds. Let sit for several weeks, then strain and bottle.
- **Ingr.:** 2 Cups white wine vinegar; 2 Tblsp toasted coriander seeds.
- **Handling and Storage Instructions:** Store in a cool, dark place. Best used within 1 year.

Mint and Cucumber Vinegar

- **P.T.:** 35 minutes
- **Acidity level:** High
- **Head Space:** 1/2 inch
- **Jar and Lid Preparation:** Sterilize jars and lids
- **Procedure:** Steep fresh mint leaves and cucumber slices in white vinegar. Let infuse, then strain and bottle.
- **Ingr.:** 2 Cups white vinegar; 1/4 Cups fresh mint leaves; 1/2 Cups cucumber, sliced.
- **Handling and Storage Instructions:** Store in a cool, dark place. Best used within 6 months.

Thyme Infused Balsamic Vinegar

- **P.T.:** 40 minutes
- **Acidity level:** High
- **Head Space:** 1/2 inch
- **Jar and Lid Preparation:** Sterilize jars and lids
- **Procedure:** Combine balsamic vinegar with fresh thyme sprigs. Allow to infuse, then strain into bottles.
- **Ingr.:** 2 Cups balsamic vinegar; 4 sprigs fresh thyme.
- **Handling and Storage Instructions:** Store in a cool, dark place. Best used within 6 months.

Garlic and Rosemary Oil

- **P.T.:** 30 minutes
- **Acidity level:** Low
- **Head Space:** 1/2 inch
- **Jar and Lid Preparation:** Sterilize jars and lids
- **Procedure:** Gently heat olive oil with minced garlic and rosemary. Cool, strain, and pour into jars.
- **Ingr.:** 2 Cups olive oil; 4 cloves garlic, minced; 4 sprigs fresh rosemary.
- **Handling and Storage Instructions:** Store in a cool, dark place. Use within 1 month.

Szechuan Pepper Oil

- **P.T.:** 30 minutes
- **Acidity level:** Low
- **Head Space:** 1/2 inch
- **Jar and Lid Preparation:** Sterilize jars and lids
- **Procedure:** Heat a neutral oil with Szechuan peppercorns. Allow to infuse, cool, then strain into bottles.
- **Ingr.:** 2 Cups neutral oil; 2 Tblsp Szechuan peppercorns.
- **Handling and Storage Instructions:** Store in a cool, dark place. Use within 2 months.

Chilli and Lime Vinegar

- **P.T.:** 35 minutes
- **Acidity level:** High
- **Head Space:** 1/2 inch
- **Jar and Lid Preparation:** Sterilize jars and lids
- **Procedure:** Infuse white vinegar with fresh chili slices and lime zest. Let sit for a few weeks, then strain and bottle.
- **Ingr.:** 2 Cups white vinegar; 4 fresh chili slices; Zest of 2 limes.
- **Handling and Storage Instructions:** Store in a cool, dark place. Best used within 6 months.

Cardamom and Orange Infused Oil

- **P.T.:** 30 minutes
- **Acidity level:** Low
- **Head Space:** 1/2 inch
- **Jar and Lid Preparation:** Sterilize jars and lids
- **Procedure:** Warm olive oil with crushed cardamom pods and orange zest. Cool, strain, and pour into jars.
- **Ingr.:** 2 Cups olive oil; 4 cardamom pods, crushed; Zest of 1 orange.
- **Handling and Storage Instructions:** Store in a cool, dark place. Use within 1 month.

Basil and Garlic Vinegar

- **P.T.:** 40 minutes
- **Acidity level:** High
- **Head Space:** 1/2 inch
- **Jar and Lid Preparation:** Sterilize jars and lids
- **Procedure:** Steep fresh basil leaves and minced garlic in white wine vinegar. Let infuse, then strain and bottle.
- **Ingr.:** 2 Cups white wine vinegar; 1/2 Cups fresh basil leaves; 4 cloves garlic, minced.
- **Handling and Storage Instructions:** Store in a cool, dark place. Best used within 6 months.

Sage and Walnut Oil

- **P.T.:** 30 minutes
- **Acidity level:** Low
- **Head Space:** 1/2 inch
- **Jar and Lid Preparation:** Sterilize jars and lids
- **Procedure:** Gently heat a neutral oil with fresh sage leaves and crushed walnuts. Cool, strain, and pour into jars.
- **Ingr.:** 2 Cups neutral oil; 1/4 Cups fresh sage leaves; 1/4 Cups crushed walnuts.
- **Handling and Storage Instructions:** Store in a cool, dark place. Use within 1 month.

Book VII: Practical Applications for Everyday Life

Meal Planning and Preparation with Preserved Foods

In the realm of home canning and preserving, the journey transcends the act of sealing flavors within jars, weaving into our daily culinary narrative. This fusion of tradition and modern convenience unfolds a plethora of opportunities for meal planning and preparation. The art of utilizing home-canned goods in everyday cooking not only marks a return to simpler, sustainable practices but also creates a symphony of convenience, health, and taste.

Envision a typical weekday where time is a luxury. Here, the convenience of home-canned goods is a beacon of simplicity. A dinner might begin with a base of pressure-canned soup, invigorated with fresh herbs and a swirl of herb-infused oil. Accompany this with crusty bread slathered in homemade garlic and rosemary butter for a meal that resonates with both comfort and nuanced flavor, effortlessly assembled.

The versatility of home-canned goods extends beyond their direct use. Picture transforming a jar of summer peach jam into a glaze for grilled meats or a vibrant dressing for salads. Here, the jar isn't just a component; it's a transformative element, elevating simple dishes to new flavor heights.

Weekend brunches could witness the delightful appearance of fruit butters and jams. Imagine pancakes or waffles, brought to life with a dollop of spiced apple butter or a drizzle of berry compote. These additions are not just flavors; they are memories of seasons past, a little jar of summer's bounty or autumn's harvest gracing your breakfast table.

Integrating home-canned items into meal planning is also a step toward dietary mindfulness. Utilizing these homemade items allows for control over ingredients, ensuring meals are free from unwanted additives and excessive sugars. It's a stride towards healthier eating, where the nutritional content is as transparent as the label on each jar.

Home-canned items also foster culinary creativity. A jar of tangy pickled vegetables can inspire a myriad of dishes: a crunchy, zesty addition to sandwiches, a vibrant component in a stir-fry, or a fresh twist in a salad. Thus, the process of canning is not just about storage but about nurturing creativity in the kitchen.

This narrative also speaks to sustainability. Using seasonally canned goods aligns with natural cycles, reducing reliance on out-of-season produce and its associated environmental impact. It's a practice that echoes the principles of local and seasonal eating, underscoring environmental responsibility.

Furthermore, these home-canned items carry cultural and familial traditions into everyday meals. Recipes passed down through generations become more than ingredients; they are stories on the dinner table, a testament to history and identity.

Emergency Preparedness: Strategies for Building a Resilient Food Supply

Envisioning a pantry stocked with a variety of home-canned goods is to see a buffer against uncertainty. The art of preserving diverse foods—fruits, vegetables, meats, and even complete meals—serves as a lifeline in times when traditional food sources may be disrupted. The process of building this resilient food supply, however, requires thoughtful planning, a keen understanding of nutritional needs, and a proactive approach to food safety and storage.

The journey begins with an assessment of dietary requirements and preferences, ensuring the pantry reflects a balance of nutrients essential for well-being. Proteins, carbohydrates, vitamins, and minerals must be considered to create a holistic and sustaining food reserve. It's about more than just sustenance; it's about maintaining a semblance of normalcy and comfort in times of distress.

Developing a skill set in both water bath and pressure canning techniques is crucial. These methods, time-tested and reliable, are the backbone of effective food preservation. Water bath canning is perfect for high-acid foods like fruits, jams, and pickles, locking in freshness and flavor. Pressure canning, on the other hand, is essential for preserving low-acid foods like meats, vegetables, and hearty stews, ensuring they remain safe and nutritious over long periods.

The narrative of emergency preparedness through canning also encompasses the art of storage and rotation. Canned goods, when stored in a cool, dark, and dry environment, can last for years. Yet, the practice of rotating your stock, using the oldest items first and replacing them with newly canned goods, ensures your pantry remains fresh and viable. This rotation is not just a practical measure; it's a rhythm, a seasonal dance that aligns with nature's bounty and the cycle of life.

In times of crisis, a well-stocked pantry becomes more than a personal asset; it transforms into a communal resource. The ability to share preserved foods with neighbors and loved ones not only strengthens bonds but also weaves a safety net of mutual support and cooperation. The act of canning and preserving, thus, transcends the individual, nurturing a sense of community resilience.

Furthermore, emergency preparedness through canning is an evolving journey. Staying abreast of the latest safety guidelines, experimenting with new recipes, and continually refining techniques is essential. Adaptability and willingness to learn are key. Whether it's experimenting with a new fruit preserve or perfecting the art of canning proteins, every jar filled is a step towards greater preparedness.

Community Engagement: Sharing Skills and Resources

At the heart of community engagement lies the sharing of skills. The knowledge of canning and preserving, often passed down through generations, holds immense value in today's fast-paced world. By organizing workshops and demonstrations, experienced canners become beacons of wisdom, illuminating the path for those eager to learn. These educational gatherings serve as more than just instructional sessions; they are communal spaces where stories are shared, bonds are formed, and a collective heritage is celebrated. They become fertile grounds for cultural exchange and intergenerational learning, where the seasoned expertise of older generations melds with the innovative ideas of the younger.

Beyond skill-sharing, these community initiatives foster a spirit of resource sharing. In neighborhoods and local groups, bulk buying of supplies can reduce costs and minimize waste. Equipment such as pressure canners, often an investment for individuals, can be shared or loaned within the community, making the practice of canning more accessible. These acts of sharing resources go beyond practical benefits; they reinforce a culture of mutual aid and collective resilience.

Community engagement in canning and preserving also opens doors to collaborative projects. Imagine a community garden where the harvest is not only shared but collectively preserved. Such initiatives not only provide a bounty of canned goods for all participants but also strengthen community ties and promote sustainable living practices. In times of surplus, these projects can extend their reach, donating preserved foods to local food banks and shelters, thus addressing food insecurity and supporting those in need.

Furthermore, it transcends the boundaries of practicality and enters the realm of celebration. Festivals and fairs dedicated to canning and preserving become jubilant events where community members showcase their creations, exchange recipes, and even engage in friendly competitions. These events are more than just showcases; they are vibrant celebrations of a community's commitment to the art of preserving food.

In the broader context, it plays a pivotal role in preserving culinary traditions. Canning recipes, often steeped in cultural heritage, become living narratives when shared within a community. These recipes tell stories – of migration, adaptation, and survival – and their preservation ensures that these stories continue to be told and remembered.

Conclusion

The Future of Home Canning and Preserving

Looking ahead, we see a future where home canning and preserving continue to thrive, bolstered by technological advancements and a growing consciousness about food sources and sustainability. The evolution of canning equipment and techniques promises to make the process more efficient, safe, and accessible to a wide audience. Innovations in pressure canning, vacuum sealing, and even smart canning appliances are on the horizon, offering the potential to reduce errors and enhance the quality of preserved foods.

As the world grapples with the implications of climate change and environmental degradation, the role of home canning and preserving in promoting sustainability becomes increasingly vital. This practice stands as a testament to resourcefulness, reducing food waste by prolonging the shelf life of produce and enabling individuals to make the most of their home gardens or local farmers' markets. In a future where the local and seasonal consumption of food becomes a necessity rather than a choice, it offers a pathway to align with these ecological imperatives.

Furthermore, the health aspects are poised to receive more attention. With a growing awareness of the impact of diet on overall well-being, more individuals are turning to home preserving as a way to control what goes into their food. The future beckons with explorations into preserving foods with lower sugar and salt content, as well as incorporating more healthful ingredients and superfoods. This evolution will continue to challenge and expand the traditional boundaries of canning recipes and techniques. The community aspect of home canning and preserving is also set to deepen. In a world where the sense of community often seems fragmented, this practice provides a powerful means of connection. From community workshops to online forums where enthusiasts share tips and recipes, the communal aspect of canning is a robust thread in the social fabric. This collective dimension is expected to grow, fostering not just the sharing of resources and knowledge but also the cultivation of local food culture and traditions.

Education and research in the field of home canning and preserving will play a crucial role in its future. As more individuals turn to this practice, the demand for comprehensive, science-backed information on safe canning methods will rise. This need presents an opportunity for institutions, from culinary schools to extension programs, to develop more in-depth educational materials and courses, ensuring that the legacy and skills of canning are passed down through generations with accuracy and enthusiasm.

Moreover, its future is likely to be marked by a resurgence of interest in heritage techniques alongside modern innovations. Fermentation, pickling, and other traditional methods are already seeing a revival, appreciated not just for their practical benefits but also for the unique flavors they impart. This renaissance of ancient practices, blended with modern food safety knowledge, creates a rich tapestry of culinary techniques for future generations to explore and enjoy.

In envisioning the future of home canning and preserving, it's also vital to consider the challenges that lie ahead. Issues such as food safety, changing climate patterns affecting crop yields, and the need for sustainable packaging materials are but a few of the hurdles that will need to be addressed.

Continuing Education: Resources and Communities for Enthusiasts

Continuing education in this field is an exhilarating adventure, blending the old with the new, tradition with innovation. In this era of information, enthusiasts have access to an unprecedented wealth of resources, ranging from online tutorials and webinars to hands-on workshops and community classes. These educational pathways are gateways to deeper knowledge and refined skills, offering enthusiasts the opportunity to explore the vast and varied landscape of canning and preserving.

The digital realm has opened up new horizons for learning. Online platforms, blogs and social media groups offer a treasure trove of information, where one can find step-by-step guides, video tutorials, and interactive webinars. These resources are invaluable, offering convenience and a broad spectrum of perspectives from around the globe. Websites dedicated to canning provide a platform for enthusiasts to stay updated with the latest techniques, safety guidelines, and innovative recipes. These digital communities also foster a sense of belonging, where individuals can share their experiences, challenges, and triumphs.

Books and publications continue to play a crucial role. From comprehensive guides authored by experts to niche books focusing on specific techniques or types of preserves, the wealth of written knowledge available to enthusiasts is immense. These publications not only offer detailed instructions but also delve into the science and history behind the practices, enriching the reader's understanding and appreciation of the craft.

Workshops and classes offered by community centers, local farms, and culinary schools are invaluable resources for hands-on learning. These sessions provide a unique opportunity to learn directly from experienced instructors, allowing for immediate feedback and guidance. They also offer the chance to connect with fellow enthusiasts, creating a network of support and camaraderie. Community canning events, where people come together to preserve large batches of seasonal produce, are not just educational but also a celebration of communal effort and shared bounty. Furthermore, food preservation clubs and societies offer structured learning opportunities and resources for members. These organizations often host regular meetings, guest lectures, and field trips, providing a structured environment for learning and exploration. Membership in these societies can also offer access to specialized equipment and bulk purchasing opportunities for canning supplies.

Conferences and symposiums on food preservation present another avenue for continuing education. These events bring together experts, hobbyists, and industry professionals, offering a platform for the exchange of ideas, research findings, and trends in the field of canning and preserving. They are not only educational but also inspirational, showcasing the innovations and future directions in the practice of food preservation.

Appendix

Troubleshooting Guide for Common Canning Issues

Embarking on the journey of home canning and preserving is akin to exploring a rich culinary landscape, filled with both rewarding harvests and occasional challenges. This troubleshooting guide is crafted to navigate you through common canning issues, offering solutions and wisdom to enhance your preserving endeavors.

1. Jar Lids Not Sealing: One of the most common issues faced in canning is jar lids failing to seal. This can be caused by several factors:

- **Faulty Lids:** Inspect lids for dents or rust. Always use new lids for each canning session to ensure a proper seal.
- **Incorrect Head Space:** Too much or too little space can prevent a proper vacuum. Ensure you're following the recipe's specified head space.
- **Residue on Jar Rim:** Any food residue on the jar rim can prevent sealing. Wipe the rim thoroughly with a clean, damp cloth before placing the lid.

2. Cloudiness in Jars: Cloudiness in jars might alarm new canners, but it can occur due to several harmless reasons:

- **Minerals in Water:** Hard water can leave mineral deposits. Consider using distilled water for canning.
- **Starch from Vegetables:** Some vegetables release starch during processing. This is normal but can be reduced by thorough washing and hot packing.
- **Spoilage:** If accompanied by off-odors or mold, cloudiness can indicate spoilage. In such cases, discard the contents.

3. Fruit Floats in Jars: Fruit floating to the top of jars can be visually unappealing, though generally harmless:

- **Packing Method:** Raw pack method often causes floating. Hot packing can help reduce this issue as pre-cooking the fruit allows it to shrink and pack more densely.
- **Syrup Density:** Adjusting the syrup density can help. Lighter syrups tend to cause more floating.

4. Siphoning or Liquid Loss: Loss of liquid during processing, known as siphoning, can occur:

- **Rapid Temperature Changes:** Avoid rapid changes in temperature. Allow the jars to cool down in the canner for a few minutes after processing.
- **Overfilling:** Ensure proper headspace to allow for food expansion.

5. Discoloration of Preserved Food: Discoloration might make the food less appealing but is often safe:

- **Light Exposure:** Store canned goods in a dark place to prevent light-induced discoloration.
- **Oxidation:** Make sure fruits are fully submerged in the liquid to prevent contact with air.

6. Crystals in Jars: Occasionally, crystals can form in canned goods:

- **Sugar Crystals in Jams and Jellies:** These are harmless but can be reduced by ensuring the sugar is fully dissolved during cooking.
- **Salt Crystals in Pickles:** Often caused by using table salt instead of pickling salt. Always use pickling or canning salt.

7. Mold Growth: Mold growth is a sign of spoilage:

- **Improper Sealing:** Check that the jars have sealed correctly. Any jars that haven't sealed should be refrigerated and used quickly or reprocessed.
- **Contamination:** Always use sterilized equipment and follow hygienic practices to minimize contamination risks.

8. Texture Changes: Texture changes in canned goods can be disappointing but are often preventable:

- **Overcooking:** Follow recommended processing times closely to prevent overcooking, which can lead to mushy textures.
- **Variety of Produce:** Use varieties of fruits and vegetables that are recommended for canning, as some varieties hold up better than others.

9. Metallic Taste: A metallic taste can sometimes be detected in canned foods:

- **Reactions with the Can:** This is often due to a chemical reaction between the food and the metal of the can. Using enamel-lined cans can help prevent this.
- **Over-Processing:** Adhering to the correct processing time and temperature can minimize this issue.

10. Fermentation: Fermentation indicated by bubbling and off-odors suggest spoilage:

- **Inadequate Processing:** Ensure you're processing for the correct time and at the right temperature.
- **Contamination:** Use sterile utensils and follow clean canning practices.

11. Seal Failure Over Time: Sometimes jars may unseal during storage:

- **Fluctuating Storage Temperatures:** Store your jars in a stable, cool, and dark environment.
- **Physical Damage:** Regularly check your stored jars for any signs of damage or unsealing.

12. Unpleasant Odors: Unpleasant odors are a clear sign of spoilage:

- **Spoilage Bacteria:** If a jar smells bad upon opening, do not taste or use the contents.

Comprehensive Resource Directory for Supplies and Further Learning

This comprehensive directory serves as a beacon, guiding enthusiasts to quality supplies and enriching educational resources, ensuring their foray into the world of canning is both successful and enjoyable.

Supplies for Home Canning and Preserving:

1. **Canning Jars and Lids:**
   - **Local Kitchen Supply Stores:** Often offer a variety of jars suitable for different types of canning.
   - **Online Retailers:** Websites like Amazon, Walmart, and specialty online stores provide a wide range of canning jars and lids.
   - **Farm Supply Stores:** These stores often carry canning supplies, particularly during harvest seasons.

2. **Pressure Canners and Water Bath Canners:**
   - **Home Goods Retailers:** Stores like Bed Bath & Beyond, Home Depot, and Lowe's often carry canners.
   - **Specialty Culinary Stores:** These stores sometimes offer high-end canners with additional features.
   - **Online Marketplaces:** Platforms like eBay can be a source for both new and used canners.

3. **Canning Utensils (Jar Lifters, Funnel, etc.):**
   - **Kitchen Specialty Stores:** Stores like Williams-Sonoma and Sur L[a] Table often carry high-quality canning utensils.
   - **Online Culinary Stores:** Websites dedicated to cooking and canning supplies.
   - **Local Hardware Stores:** These stores sometimes stock canning utensils especially in rural areas.

4. **Labeling and Packaging Materials:**
   - **Craft Stores:** Stores like Michaels and Hobby Lobby offer a variety o[f] labeling and packaging options.
   - **Online Printing Services:** Websites like Vistaprint or Avery allow fo[r] custom label creation.
   - **Office Supply Stores:** Staples and Office Depot offer basic labels an[d] markers.

Educational Resources for Canning and Preserving:

1. **Online Courses and Webinars:**
   - **Coursera, Udemy, and Skillshare:** Offer courses ranging from beginne[r] to advanced levels in canning and food preservation.
   - **Extension Services Webinars:** Many university extension services offe[r] free or low-cost webinars on canning.

2. **Books and Publications:**
   - **"Ball Complete Book of Home Preserving":** A comprehensive guid[e] covering a wide range of canning topics.
   - **"The All New Ball Book of Canning and Preserving":** Offers bot[h] classic and contemporary canning recipes.
   - **Local Libraries and Bookstores:** Often stock a variety of books o[n] canning and preserving.

3. **Blogs and Online Forums:**
   - **"Food in Jars":** A popular blog with recipes and tips.
   - **"Simply Canning":** Offers practical advice and tutorials.
   - **Online Communities:** Platforms like Reddit and Facebook have active canning groups where enthusiasts share advice and experiences.

4. **Workshops and Local Classes:**
   - **Community Centers and Adult Education Programs:** Often offer canning classes.
   - **Kitchen Supply Stores:** Sometimes host canning workshops.
   - **Agricultural Fairs and Festivals:** Can be a source for hands-on learning and demonstrations.

5. **Extension Services and Local Agricultural Agencies:**
   - **Cooperative Extension Services:** Offer resources, workshops, and printed materials on canning and food safety.
   - **Agricultural Experiment Stations:** Sometimes provide testing services for canning recipes and techniques.

6. **Conferences and Symposiums:**
   - **Mother Earth News Fairs:** Offer workshops and presentations on a variety of homesteading topics, including canning.
   - **State and County Fairs:** Often have canning competitions and demonstrations

Detailed Glossary of Canning and Preserving Terms

- **Acidification:** The process of adding acid (like lemon juice or vinegar) to foods to lower their pH. This is essential in water bath canning to prevent the growth of harmful bacteria.

- **Botulism:** A potentially fatal foodborne illness caused by toxins produced by the bacterium Clostridium botulinum. Proper canning methods are crucial to prevent botulism.

- **Canning Salt:** A fine-grained salt without additives such as iodine or anti-caking agents, used in pickling and canning to prevent cloudiness or discoloration.

- **Cold Pack Method (Raw Pack):** Filling jars with raw, unheated food. Liquid is then added, leaving appropriate headspace, before processing.

- **Headspace:** The space left between the top of the food and the rim of the jar. This space allows for food expansion during processing and is crucial for creating a vacuum seal.

- **Hot Pack Method:** Pre-cooking food before placing it into jars for processing. This method often results in a better quality product with less floating and more compact storage.

- **Jelly Bag:** A fine mesh bag used for straining juice from fruits when making jellies. It ensures a clear jelly by removing pulp and sediment.

- **Low-Acid Foods:** Foods with a pH value higher than 4.6, including most vegetables, some fruits, and all meats. They require pressure canning for safe preservation.

- **Pectin:** A natural substance found in fruits, used as a gelling agent in making jellies and jams. It's often added in powdered or liquid form to achieve the desired set.

- **Pressure Canning:** A method used for preserving low-acid foods, involving a pressure canner to achieve high temperatures (240°F or 116°C) necessary to destroy botulinum spores.

- **Processing Time:** The length of time jars are boiled in a water bath or pressure canner, essential for ensuring food safety.

- **Quart:** A unit of volume measurement in canning, equivalent to 2 pints, 4 cups, or approximately 1 liter.

- **Seal:** The airtight closure formed when the lid of a canning jar is vacuum-sealed onto the jar, preventing air and bacteria from entering.

- **Siphoning:** The phenomenon where liquid is drawn out of the jars during processing, often due to rapid temperature changes or overfilling.

- **Sterilization:** The process of eliminating all forms of bacteria, fungi, and other microorganisms from canning jars and equipment, typically through boiling.

- **Vacuum Seal:** The seal formed in a jar when the contents are processed and cooled, causing the lid to be sucked down and creating an airtight, safe environment for food preservation.

- **Water Bath Canning:** A method of processing high-acid foods (like fruits and pickles) in a large pot of boiling water, suitable for foods with a pH of 4.6 or lower.

- **Zest:** The outer peel of citrus fruits, often used in canning recipes to add flavor. It is important to avoid the white pith, which can add bitterness.

Index

A

- Acidic Foods Canning, 53
- Advanced Preservation and Storage, 143
- Alternative Preservation Methods, 99

B

- Basics of Canning and Preserving, 25
- Book I: Foundations of Canning and Preserving, 25
- Book II: Water Bath Canning, 31
- Book III: Pressure Canning, 65
- Book IV: Alternative Preservation Methods, 99
- Book V: Advanced Preservation and Storage, 143
- Book VI: Special Topics and Recipes, 149
- Book VII: Practical Applications for Everyday Life, 211
- Bourbon-Infused Cherries, 52
- Brandied Cherries, 44
- Bread and Butter Pickles, 57
- Building a Varied and Nutritious Prepper's Pantry, 143

C

- Canning Vegetables and Soups, 67
- Classic Beef Stew, 67
- Classic Duck Confit, 82
- Cold Smoked Cheese, 140
- Combining Foods: Creating Balanced Meals in a Jar, 87
- Community Engagement: Sharing Skills and Resources, 214
- Comprehensive Resource Directory for Supplies and Further Learning, 226
- Conclusion, 217
- Coriander Seed Vinegar, 204
- Cranberry-Orange Relish, 58
- Creating Balanced Meals in a Jar, 87

- Cream of Asparagus Soup, 75
- Cucumber and Mint Chutney, 60
- Cultured Mustard, 109
- Curried Pickled Cauliflower, 130
- Curried Lamb Stew, 79

D

- Dehydrating Fruits, Vegetables, and Meats, 110
- Detailed Glossary of Canning and Preserving Terms, 229
- Dill Garlic Cucumbers, 54
- Dried Blueberries, 119

E

- Emergency Preparedness: Strategies for Building a Resilient Food Supply, 212
- Essential Equipment and Their Uses, 25

F

- Fermenting Foods: Health Benefits and Basic Recipes, 99
- Fiery Jalapeño Pickles, 124
- Fig and Port Wine Jam, 188
- Filtration and Sterilization Techniques, 28
- Finding Quality Ingredients for Optimal Preservation, 27
- French Ratatouille Preserve, 166

G

- Garlic and Herb Seasoned Tomatoes, 117
- Garlic Dill Green Beans, 60
- Ginger-Pear Jelly, 34
- Ginger-Pickled Daikon Radish, 125
- Green Tomato and Apple Chutney, 190
- Green Tomato Chutney, 55

H

- Hearty Vegetable Soup, 67
- Herb-Infused Pork Chops, 78
- Herbed Chicken Thighs, 84

- Honeyed Pear Preserves, 44

I

- Indian Mango Chutney, 164
- Introduction, 17
- Introduction to Water Bath Canning: Principles and Practices, 31
- Italian Marinated Artichokes, 165

J

- Jambalaya, 95
- Japanese Umeboshi (Pickled Plums), 165

K

- Kiwi-Lime Preserve, 39

L

- Lemon and Rosemary Olives, 61
- Lentil Soup with Vegetables, 69
- Lemon-Thyme Jelly, 153
- Low-Sugar, Low-Salt, and Allergen-Free Recipes, 149

M

- Mango & Saffron Marmalade, 33
- Mango-Lime Chutney, 53
- Mead, Poultry, and Seafood Preservation Techniques, 77
- Mediterranean Lamb Stew, 96
- Miso Fermented Vegetables, 104
- Moroccan Chickpea and Vegetable Stew, 87
- Moroccan Preserved Lemons, 164

N

- Non-Traditional Preservation Methods, 99

O

- Overview of Canning and Preserving: A Historical Perspective, 19

P

- Pear and Ginger Chutney, 59
- Pickled Asparagus Spears, 127

- Pickled Cherry Tomatoes, 125
- Pickled Pearl Onions, 128
- Pickled Radishes with Peppercorns, 129
- Pickling: Beyond Cucumbers - Exploring Variety, 121
- Pineapple-Cilantro Jam, 39
- Pineapple Tepache, 105
- Plum-Star Anise Jam, 40
- Pork Carnitas, 85
- Preserving Fruits and Tomatoes: From Orchard to Jar, 43
- Preserving Herbs and Spices: Oils, Vinegars, and Infusions, 194

Q

- Quince-Pear Butter, 51

R

- Red Currant-Chile Jelly, 41
- Red Onion Marmalade, 56
- Resources and Communities for Enthusiasts, 219
- Rosemary Infused Olive Oil, 194
- Rustic Grape Jam, 47
- Rustic Pear Preserve, 150

S

- Safety Protocols and Hygiene in Home Canning, 21
- Savory Bacon Jam, 193
- Savory Mushroom Pâté, 152
- Seasonal and Bulk Canning: Strategies for Year-Round Preparation, 146
- Smoking and Curing Meats: Traditional and Modern Methods, 131
- Spiced Blueberry Jam, 33
- Spiced Corn Relish, 58
- Spiced Peach Slices, 43
- Spicy Bean and Rice Burrito Filling, 93
- Spicy Carrot Chutney, 161
- Spicy Tomato Chutney, 46

- Sun-Dried Tomato Tapenade, 157
- Sweet Pickled Red Cabbage, 126
- Sweet and Spicy Zucchini Pickles, 55
- Sweet Pepper Jelly, 163
- Sweet Potato Dog Treats, 111

T

- The Future of Home Canning and Preserving, 217
- The Rising Importance of Self-Sufficiency in the 21st Century, 17
- Troubleshooting Guide for Common Canning Issues, 223
- Turkish Eggplant Pickle, 170

U

- Understanding Pressure Canning: The Science and Method, 65

V

- Vanilla-Infused Plums, 47
- Vegetarian Borscht, 92
- Vegetarian Quinoa Chili, 88
- Vietnamese Pickled Vegetables, 130

W

- Water Bath Canning, 31

Z

- Zesty Lemon Zest, 112
- Zucchini and Lemon Marmalade, 191

Abbreviations

Minute(s): min.

Hour(s): hr.

Spoon(s) / Teaspoon(s): tsp

Table spoon(s): Tblsp

Pint: pt.

Quart: qt.

Gallon: gal.

Fluid: fl.

Once: oz.

Pounds: lb.

Measurement Conversion Table

Volume Measurements

US Measurement	Metric Measurement
1 teaspoon (tsp)	5 milliliters (ml)
1 tablespoon (tbsp)	15 milliliters (ml)
1 fluid ounce (fl oz)	30 milliliters (ml)
1 cup (Cups)	240 milliliters (ml)
1 pint (2 Cs)	470 milliliters (ml)
1 quart (4 Cs)	0.95 liters (L)
1 gallon (16 Cs)	3.8 liters (L)

Weight Measurements

US Measurement	Metric Measurement
1 ounce (oz)	28 grams (g)
1 pound (lb)	450 grams (g)
1 pound (lb)	0.45 kilograms (kg)

Length Measurements

US Measurement	Metric Measurement
1 inch (in)	2.54 centimeters (cm)
1 foot (ft)	30.48 centimeters (cm)
1 foot (ft)	0.3048 meters (m)
1 yard (yd)	0.9144 meters (m)

Temperature Conversions

Fahrenheit (°F)	Celsius (°C)
32°F	0°C
212°F	100°C
Formula: (°F - 32) x 0.5556 = °C	Formula: (°C x 1.8) + 32 = °F

Oven Temperature Conversions

US Oven Term	Fahrenheit (°F)	Celsius (°C)
Very Slow	250°F	120°C
Slow	300-325°F	150-165°C
Moderate	350-375°F	175-190°C
Moderately Hot	400°F	200°C
Hot	425-450°F	220-230°C
Very Hot	475-500°F	245-260°C

Made in the USA
Las Vegas, NV
09 November 2024

11439006R00136